Praise for *#LookUp*

P9-DGE-409

"Judy Stoffel's book, *#LookUp*, offers parents factual, practical, and developmentally appropriate approaches to managing your 'digital family life' in the age of digital nativism. As a child advocate, nonprofit leader, and veteran mom of two young adults, I am glad to see Judy's call to action for digital citizenship. Since parents are a child's first and best teacher, it is up to us to begin to teach our children what skills, purpose, and boundaries are necessary as they learn to use technology for academics, work, communication, and fun."

—Michele Strasz, Catalyst for Action Consultants, 2019

"As a physician and father of two teenage boys, Judy's discussion of the physiological and psychological effects of screen use on our children appeals to me both logically and emotionally. *#LookUp* comes at a perfect time for our family as we try to rein in screen time, deepen relationships with one another, and raise content, independent, empathic young men. Judy presents practical solutions that will empower any family striving to 'look up' more!"

—Nate Pitner, M.D., Ph.D.

"*#LookUp* is an absolute must-read for every parent regardless of the ages of their children or how far down the parenting road they have traveled. The life-changing and research-based information in this book will inform parents of the potentially detrimental effects that technology can have on their kids. Stoffel does an amazing job of sharing scientific information in a compelling manner that inspires the reader toward change. She also includes a myriad of practical and attainable solutions to take back our kids and our families from the addictive smorgasbord of tech devices that threaten to side-track us all from the things that matter the most in life; namely family, friends, and community. I highly recommend this book to anyone who desires healthier habits around technology for their kids and their families. #LookUp should be sent home from the hospital with new parents and used in parenting classes designed for parents of teens. It is inspiring and edifying on many levels!"

—Tiffany McIntosh, BA education, BA sociology,
MA curriculum and instruction;
parenting instructor, former middle school teacher,
and mother of four children

"I commend Judy Stoffel for shining a light on the ever-growing problem of 'text neck', which is often not even thought of when addressing our technology problems in our children. As a doc-tor of Chiropractic, I used to think that when iPads and tablets came out that the heavy backpack problem would be solved. I was wrong. Our kids are still carrying too heavy of backpacks and now they are spending hours each day hunched over their devices. It is causing major problems to our children's spines. I am seeing more and more children coming in with neck pain and headaches dues to their posture. Unfortunately, many more problems won't be realized until our children are older. The time to deal with this is now, when they are young. Thank you, Judy, for addressing this topic!"

—Dr. Aaron Morland, owner and practitioner of
Valeo Health and Wellness Center

"Powerful, practical, and solid advice on the impact screens are having on our children's brains and bodies. Judy Stoffel's research and exper-tise will make you challenge the status quo and change the way you think about your devices."

—Joy Hanson Fischer, LICSW

"*#LookUp* offers comprehensive research behind the physical and psychological effects of screen use, a needed resource as our parenting generation witnesses technology addiction developing in kids in real time. Judy Stoffel's book should prompt every mom or dad to re-evaluate household norms. Her practical, bold tips will motivate change."

—Anne Carraux, mother of four children

"I applaud Ms. Stoffel for acknowledging all the amazing benefits of our devices and also showing us the cost we are paying for this connectivity. She's not asking us to take away our kids' phones, just to be more thoughtful on how they are used. I've been a high school teacher for twenty-six years, and the societal impacts are especially alarming. It's sad to look into our school cafeteria and see so many students looking down at their phones. Just five years ago, they would have been talking and laughing with each other. The $300 million, 10-year government study on kids and screens that Ms. Stoffel references is HUGE and another sign parents do need to take this issue seriously. Her solutions are also a great resource for teachers of all grades, and I will be using many of them in my classroom."

—Tamara Sather, high school teacher

"We have access to unlimited information through the multitude of devices at our fingertips. This book perfectly summarizes both the gift and the challenge that presents and offers practical advice to this problem. It's impossible to achieve outstanding results if we are distracted by our devices, whether that is in the classroom, the boardroom, or our personal relationships. Ms. Stoffel is correct in her assessment that the big Silicon Valley monopolies make money when they sell our attention to their advertisers. Rather than waiting for that model to change, it's up to us to start making changes in our own homes. This book offers great solutions to achieve a healthy balance in your life and the lives of your children. It starts with you. Take charge."

—Anne Loughrey, founder of "Been There, Read That" blog, Certified Public Accountant, 30-year business professional, working mother of three children

"As a teacher for nineteen years, I have noticed negative behavioral changes in students starting as young as five years old. I do believe the proliferation of technology is a big contributor to this, and I suspect many parents may be using screens to occupy or "babysit" their children. Ms. Stoffel's advice and solutions to have more intentional use of screens will help get parents on the right track. This book is very well-written, and I plan to recommend *#LookUp* to all my parents."

—Amy Lindahl, cross-categorical special education teacher K-2

"The author has compiled a great deal of research to create an impetus for parents to start a program to limit their family screen use. It is definitely not an easy task, but the reasons to do this are scary and real. I especially liked the solutions chapter—so many good ideas to get started. Even though I am not as attached to my screens as many young people today, I am instituting the 'no screens two hours before bedtime' rule for myself."

—Mary Welch, retired school teacher, 40 years' experience

"As a teacher of seventeen years and mom of thirteen years, I found the information in this book very beneficial. A lot of research that helps one understand what the brain is doing as it connects to technology is included in this book. In teaching today, students want to know "why." *#LookUp* is full of information about why it is important to be informed and to control these super computers that our children have available. There were many wonderful suggestions of what steps to take as we guide our young people in balancing technology with real life."

—Barb Meinert, 4th grade teacher, St. Hubert School

"The beauty of this book is that Judy Stoffel presents not only the pros and cons of the pervasive screen presence in our lives but does not leave the reader there. She proposes many solutions that make living in this information age increasingly more healthy and balanced. As a mother of nine, I have witnessed a tremendous challenge evolve from our oldest to our youngest with regards to screen addiction and age-appropriate information available. Judy's in-depth research arms us with proof to the psychological, emotional, and physiological harm brought on by overuse of screens. Technology is here to stay, but this book is a great weapon toward protecting ourselves and our families!"

—Denise Westerhaus, mother of nine children

"This is a wonderful book that Ms. Stoffel has written! As a teacher, particularly in kindergarten, I viewed technology as a useful tool but never felt the need to use much technology in the classroom. It was important for me to connect eye to eye with my students, touch to touch, and really listen to what they had to say. The research she presents supports this as well. Ms. Stoffel's "Everything You Learned in Kindergarten Analogy" was clever, and perhaps all kindergarten teachers should enhance their curriculum with these digital lessons given the world we live in today. I also like the author's comments on empathy, humility, and respect. Her family media plan is realistic and very straightforward; it should be an objective for every family to put a media plan in place."

—Mary Thomas, elementary education teacher

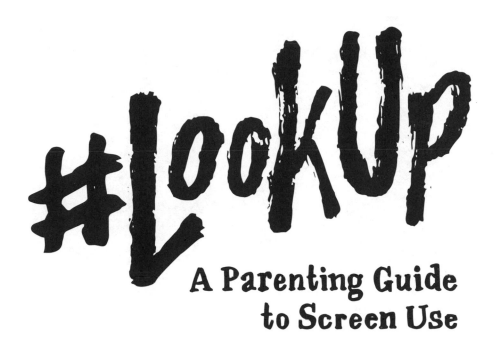

A Parenting Guide
to Screen Use

#LookUp

A Parenting Guide to Screen Use

JUDY STOFFEL

WISE INK
MINNEAPOLIS

#LookUp: A Parenting Guide to Screen Use © 2019 Judy Stoffel
All rights reserved. No part of this book may be reproduced in any
form whatsoever, by photography or xerography or by any other
means, by broadcast or transmission, by translation into any kind
of language, nor by recording electronically or otherwise, without
permission in writing from the author, except by a reviewer, who
may quote brief passages in critical articles or reviews.

ISBN: 978-1-63489-201-8
Library of Congress Catalog Number: 2019930532
Printed in the United States of America
First Printing: 2019
23 22 21 20 19   5 4 3 2 1

Book design by Athena Currier

Wise Ink Creative Publishing.
807 Broadway Street NE, Suite 46
Minneapolis, MN 55413
wiseink.com

To order, visit www.itascabooks.com
or call 1-800-901-3480. Reseller discounts available.

This book is dedicated to my cute little dad, Gerald Weigel, a humble member of the Greatest Generation. He was an ordinary man whose life was laced with the markings of greatness. Throughout his life he stayed true to the values of honesty, respect, integrity, hard work, and personal responsibility. The virtues and lessons he taught me are woven throughout the pages of this book. I am so proud that this ordinary man was my extraordinary father.

"They came of age during the Great Depression and the Second World War and went on to build modern America—men and women whose everyday lives of duty, honor, achievement and courage gave us the world we have today." —Tom Brokaw, *The Greatest Generation*

Contents

Preface

Since I'm not an engineer, scientist, or computer programmer, some of you may be wondering what qualifications I have for writing a book on technology. I am a certified public accountant (CPA), and my twenty-year career has been in the business world. I've worked for large multinational companies in treasury, finance, audit, accounting, and reporting. I've worked with boards of directors, Wall Street analysts, rating agencies, bankers, and brokers. I've executed mergers and acquisitions from all sides, including due diligence, financial modeling, synergy analysis, and integration. I've completed multimillion-dollar deals involving debt offerings, stock sales, and stock repurchases. I've managed over a billion dollars in cash and investments. I am obsessed with the stock market and understand the drivers of corporate stock prices and the economy. Most relevant to this topic, I understand incentive stock options, executive pay, and bonus compensation. So what does this business experience have to do with our kids using screens?

First and foremost, this is a business problem! Tech monopolies like Google and Facebook only succeed in the long run if they make money. And how do they make money when consumers aren't paying to open up a Facebook account or use Google's search engine? They run ads and hope we buy their products. In essence, they are selling our attention and will do anything they can to get us hooked. That's their definition of success.

But what makes me most qualified to write this book is the other, much more important, role I hold—I am a mother. I have twenty-nine years of experience raising children. I know their stages, how they grow, what they need to thrive, and what fails. I am fiercely protective of my kids, and I'll do anything to keep them safe and teach them how to be healthy and happy.

I'm not going to let a twenty-five-year-old, rich Silicon Valley engineer take control of my children's eyes and fingers. They're mine, and I choose to use them for good. I choose to have them look me in the eye and have a deep conversation. I choose to have them look up and see all the beauty of nature around them. I choose to have them use their hands to work hard and help build better communities.

I'm not going to let them get glued to their screens just because the big businesses need their engagement to make money. I want to let those businesses fail and start over with a model that doesn't involve addicting my kids and their friends. I'm not going to hold my breath and expect immediate change; it is going to take years before these companies figure out a new income stream and pay structure that don't involve selling our attention. But I hope that this book serves as a call to action for parents to step up and make a commitment to conquer this digital beast, to rein in screen time for ourselves and our children before too much damage is done.

> "If you bungle raising your children, I don't think
> whatever else you do matters very much."
>
> —Jacqueline Kennedy Onassis

Introduction

During our local church's small group study, a woman had her iPhone sitting in the middle of the table. She pointed at the Apple logo on her phone and said, "Isn't it ironic that we are talking about the devil tempting Adam and Eve with an apple, and thousands of years later the biggest temptation for us and our children is another apple?"

There are also non-biblical references to apples representing evil, particularly in fairy tales. One of the most well-known examples is the Brothers Grimm tale "Snow White," in which an evil stepmother offers a princess a poisonous apple that puts her to sleep, only for her to be awakened by true love's kiss. In Greek mythology, three goddesses' fight over an apple inadvertently starts the Trojan War.

This isn't a book about religion, and I don't mean to imply Steve Jobs was the devil. But that comment sparked my interest in our cell phone usage and the temptations that we, as a society, are succumbing to. This book came to life after extensive research and personal interviews convinced me that our devices are wreaking havoc on our children's health and happiness, and they are stressing parents out. I needed to transfer this knowledge to other parents for them to make the best-informed decisions for their children and family.

Don't get me wrong—I have a cell phone, an iPad, and a computer. My children have devices as well. We have the gadgets in our home, but we're not tethered to them. I'm not asking you to give up your screens, just to learn healthy habits so you can own your phone without your phone owning you. The benefits of the internet, and cell phones in particular, are life changing, and I will briefly touch on those in my first chapter.

Getting back to Steve Jobs, it's particularly interesting that he chose for his company's logo an image of an apple with a bite taken out (or shall I say a *byte* taken out?). He could have easily used an unblemished, whole, lush, red, juicy apple like we give to our teachers, one that represents all things good. But Jobs chose one that shows temptation as the victor.

In the decade or so since the iPhone first came out, we have fundamentally changed almost every facet of our daily lives, particularly how we communicate (text) and what we do for entertainment (stream). This change has been swift, universal, and radical regardless of your age, where you live, or your socioeconomic status. This unprecedented adoption of technology kicked off the largest uncontrolled experiment on humankind that's ever been done. That's not just my opinion—many experts agree as well. We are the lab mice, texting, scrolling, binge watching, and posting all day long, while the research teams that work at Google and Facebook track our every move. The trajectory of this runaway use of screens is looking vaguely familiar.

There are a few things in society, like cigarettes and gambling, that are unequivocally proven to be addictive. It wouldn't be a stretch to add two more things to this list—in my opinion, our number one recreational drug of choice is a close race between sugar and screens. In my chapter on the risks of technology, you will see the parallel between addictive substances and our screen activity.

I'm going to teach you some cool new buzzwords you can bring out at the dinner table with your kiddos: plasticity, dopamine, cortisol, melatonin, serotonin, monkey brain, switch tasking, digital dementia, Pygmalion effect, blue light, and more. I don't want you to be scared screenless—just armed with the most recent research available to strive for a healthy relationship with technology.

I will also discuss a few of the human virtues that are quickly vanishing before our eyes. Many parents today seem to value achievement and trophies over kindness and empathy. We teach our kids how to get good grades and how to get into the right college, but often forget to teach them to care. Our kids are so busy recording their lives for their Facebook or Instagram audience that they forget to live them.

Before cell phones, parents would schedule play dates with friends, and when children were at home, they were with their family. Family time and friend time had a clear divide. With smartphones, kids' friends are there whenever they have their phones, which can mean "virtual socializing" 24-7. That's great for many kids to stay connected, but take the average of seven hours a day on screens[1] and there's very little family time left.

This would be easier to take if our kids were actually happy, but all the data point to a direct correlation between screentime/social media use and depression and anxiety. We are living in a state of emergency from the minute we wake up until the minute we go to sleep. Daily life is moving at dizzying speeds—so much information is thrown at us, it's almost like taking a sip of water out of a firehose. Our bodies are not designed to be in this fight-or-flight state all day long. We're drowning in information and starving for practical ways to unplug for both ourselves and our children.

Here's an anecdotal description from a mother I interviewed on the familial and societal changes she has seen with technology today.

"We purchased cell phones for our five children at various ages, ranging from thirteen to eighteen. I have seen [a very] negative impact [on] their behavior. From not being 100 percent 'present' in family conversations and activities to having a reduced social need to get together with friends in person, the antisocial changes are disarming. Gone are the days when my kids [would] open up the board game closet, build family puzzles, or shoot hoops in the driveway without me setting boundaries for their devices and redirecting their free time. My older adult children feel sorry for their younger siblings and their friends who [had] access to smartphones earlier than [the previous] generation. They see addiction, isolation, narcissistic habits, and bullying in the younger generation, not to mention their early access to inappropriate content. [It seems this] topic is part of every parent-to-parent conversation these days. I truly hope the pendulum will shift back as millennials see the destruction these devices are having on the next generation."

This screen madness is becoming so commonplace that we are forgetting to question it. That stops now. It's time to fight for our children's future and reject the status quo. While the original invention may have been a simple mobile phone, kids are not really using their cell phones to call people. It is a highly addictive supercomputer in their pocket, so let's call it what it is.

> My goal in this book is to prove that your cell phone can be indispensable without being addictive.

There's no undo button when it comes to raising kids, and your decisions from early on will affect many facets of their development. This truly may be the biggest issue you will ever face as a parent, and I'm calling you to be brave and take action. I will get you started with my version of an SOS—solutions over screens. This book offers you fifty simple, sensible, straightforward, and practical ways to rein in screen time. Screens are tools, and my solutions don't involve banning phones altogether—just teaching our kids how to use them in a reasonable manner at an appropriate age.

I will show you how to put together a Family Media Plan and have "The Talk" with your kids. Usually, this is code for the birds and the bees, but in this day and age we need to expand the talk to include pornography and screen usage.

We need our kids to ultimately be able to police themselves and make the right decisions when they're alone in their college dorm rooms, when no one's looking. By explaining to them the "why" behind our decisions on technology, we allow them to see our choices not just as house rules but as healthy habits to keep up when they move out. We don't want them fighting off a screen addiction by white-knuckling their way through the day.

Let's all agree that our cell phones and devices are life-changing—there are amazing benefits to all this connectivity. Electronic devices are not going away, and there is a place for them in our daily life. The challenge is to change the way we interact with them so that they are serving us, not the other way around. We must tame this beast, this highly portable, three-by-five-inch rectangular screen with unimaginable capabilities.

My goal in this book is to prove that your cell phone can be indispensable without being addictive. We just need to institute some daily routines to attain that "Goldilocks" relationship with technology. Not too much, not too little—just right.

Chapter I

"The Bennies"

The benefits (aka "bennies") of digital platforms in today's society are undeniable. In fact, they are so obvious that I don't want to spend much time on the topic. I'll pretend I'm Facebook and give you the highlight reel.

The little box that lives in our pocket is far beyond just a convenience; for many of us, our very occupation requires us to be on some kind of a device all day long. It's our clock, our GPS, our camera, our computer, our weather station, and our lifeline to our extended circle of family, friends, schoolmates, and coworkers. If used moderately and appropriately, the device can be useful for both parents and children.

This magical device can satisfy our every whim to keep us entertained or informed. Huge companies are being built almost overnight to accommodate our digital requests. Gone are the days when a significant capital investment was required to support brick-and-mortar locations that drew people in. Now, you can sell to millions without owning any assets whatsoever. Uber, the largest taxi company, owns no cars. Airbnb, the world's largest accommodation provider, owns no real estate. Facebook, the world's most popular social media platform, creates no content.

Really, anyone with a computer and an imagination can get the ball rolling. (Hint, hint, millennials—get those thinking caps on.)

The way I see it, these societal changes and the ways we use our devices fall into four main categories: communication, entertainment, information, and functionality. Let's start with how we interact with others.

Communication

Thanks to many of these pop-up entities, it's never been easier to communicate with friends, relatives, and coworkers. The world is our playground and the internet melts away the miles. Snail mail, fax, phone calls, and in-person conversations have been replaced by texts, tweets, kik, snaps, posts, messages, video chat, and FaceTime. I'm a busy mom, and it's very efficient to be able to send a quick text to a group of local mothers on carpool issues, playdates, or school questions. We can also connect and reach out with love and support to those in crisis situations via amazing applications like CaringBridge, GoFundMe, or Meal Train.

Social media sites in particular are life-changing, allowing us to share photos, life updates, or personal observations about the world. Educational portals have dramatically enhanced the way parents, teachers, and students can communicate and share information. With one click of our mouse, we can obtain information on missing assignments, attendance, upcoming tests, grades, and school news. Since I live in Minnesota and we frequently have no school due to weather conditions, cold (minus fifty degrees!), or snow (two feet!), having an easy way to access information about school closings at 6:00 a.m. is invaluable. And man, do our kids here love snow days! In fact, as much as I run a very structured household, on snow days all the rules are thrown out the window and my kiddos can play outside in the snow for hours, sip hot chocolate with marshmallows to their heart's content, sleep all day, eat junk food all day, watch TV all day, or play video games all day. No rules on snow days!

Entertainment

As a society, we're constantly goofing around on our screens to keep us entertained—they bring the word "toy" to a level even Santa's elves couldn't imagine. We stream movies, listen to music, play video games, watch YouTube videos, read on our Kindle, and scroll through our social media accounts. As of June 2018, Facebook had cemented its worldwide dominance with 2.2 billion active users. Next in line was YouTube with 1.8 billion users, and Instagram with 800 million.[1] Netflix in, Blockbuster out.

Information

The electronic world library is at our fingertips, and what we can search is almost limitless. For children, this provides an obvious advantage for homework. The World Wide Web is an effective tool to do research, practice math problems, submit college applications, consult the dictionary, and translate between languages. Many older folks used to watch Sunday morning mass on television; now religious access has dramatically increased, with online Bibles, daily prayers and devotionals, inspirational videos, and even resources like MassTimes.org, which gives upcoming mass times for any zip code.

Telematics (black box) car insurance use has increased dramatically over recent years. The app will electronically monitor your driving and send the information to your insurance carrier. If it shows you're a safe and reliable driver, you could save on your car insurance premiums. Voice-powered assistants like Siri, Echo, or Google glasses dramatically improve the information available to all users, and voice-activated commands prove especially valuable to the elderly, sick, blind, or handicapped. Digital devices such as an iPad or computer can be lifesavers for children with autism or other challenges, since they can aid in concentration and focus.

Functionality/Efficiency

What we can buy, book, track, and schedule on our phones is absolutely unbelievable. Besides their obvious functionality as our camera and local weather personality, our phones are always able to tell us the current time, beam up our daily calendar, and give us directions on command. If we don't drive or we want a night out on the town, no problem—Uber and Lyft will pick us up in minutes. Want to split a cab fare? Venmo me. Our local travel agent has big competition with sites like Expedia, Airbnb, and VRBO. One of the best enhancements of these online travel sites is being able to read reviews from former users who can recommend a particular site.

Retail therapy has taken on a whole new dimension in the digital era, far surpassing the draw of the local mall or the Home Shopping Network. Almost any consumer product is available online, with the market largely dominated by Amazon. Etsy has provided an amazing space to match up crafters with customers. If we need money to pay for all these retail purchases, we can search the web for jobs through Monster or Indeed. Social media and streaming sites like Snapchat, Hulu, and Spotify are being used to hire new employees, particularly in the target market of sixteen- to twenty-four-year-olds. McDonald's in Australia recently used Snapchat to get new hires via a ten-second "Snaplication"—fast food, fast jobs. Once we get that job and make money, we can use the virtual teller that lives in our phone to do our online banking, including paying, depositing our paycheck, and monitoring our balances. And once we're done buying stuff, we don't even have to run a local garage sale to declutter—we can sell our used items on Craigslist or eBay.

We can even buy perishables online. Food delivery has far surpassed pizza or Chinese food delivery—we can now purchase our weekly groceries online through a myriad of regional fulfillment vendors. And even those perishables have had their life cycle affected by technology—a promising new advancement in the agricultural industry is the use of drones to provide precise and efficient use of fertilizer and water.

Societal Changes

There have also been many positive societal shifts for our children as a result of technology. Many children are actually physically safer now that their phone is their best friend—they have no reason to leave the house or even their bedroom. They don't need to meet up at the pizza parlor to get together; they can chat online or meet on "Houseparty." According to *iGen* author Jean Twenge, "A twelfth grader now goes out less than an eighth grader did in 2005. [. . .] More and more teens are leaving high school never having had a paying job, driven a car by themselves, gone out on a date, had sex, or tried alcohol."[2]

And now comes the *but* . . . While our kids may be physically safer and growing up later, the gleaming benefits from our devices come at a very large cost to growing children. The rewards we get from being constantly connected are really starting to undermine the fabric of society, not to mention our children's mental and physical health. Most of us want to hear good news about our bad habits, but this isn't one of those times. As much as I love my rose-colored glasses and usually see the glass as half full, even I can't overlook the potential consequences of kids using screens. I don't want to be a downer, but let's examine the risks so you can make informed decisions for yourself and your children.

Chapter II

The Risks: Medical Side Effects of Too Much Screen Time

Many of us have our eyes glued to screens from the moment we get out of bed to the moment we close our eyes at the end of the day. We are digitally tethered to our devices, seemingly unaware of the price we pay to live in this electronic world—especially to growing children. It's becoming so normal that we forget to even question if this is healthy. But in reality, we need to begin a discourse about this issue. We need to really "see" the most recent research on what screens are doing to our children's mental and physical health, and the impact they have on our relationships and communities.

I have two primary concerns with our children using digital devices:

> **1. What is happening to their bodies and their brains.**
> Excessive screen time can change children on both a physiological and a psychological level, leading to a myriad of health concerns I will discuss in this chapter.

2. What is not happening to their bodies and their brains.
By spending so much time on screens, children are missing out on key activities that help build a healthy and long-lasting brain and body, and they can lose out on critical interpersonal relationships. There is a profound loss of opportunities that comes from very little time being devoted to reading, sports, music, face-to-face conversations, volunteering, praying, and spending quiet time alone with their thoughts. Having a variety of experiences and activities is a crucial component to children's long-term health and happiness.

A lot of parents dismiss the negative effects of their kid's cell phones. "People thought the same thing about the invention of the television in our era," they say, "and we turned out okay."

Let me emphasize: there is *no* comparison between using a television screen and using a cell phone screen. Phones are portable, and most televisions are not. We left the house for school, work, ball games, and the pizza parlor, and the television stayed at home. We couldn't possibly bring it with us. Most houses back then only had one television, so even if you were home, you split time with your parents and other siblings. The sheer portability of cell phones and the fact that we don't need to share them make them so much more addicting. They have become almost like an appendage, following our kids everywhere all the time. In addition, the close proximity of a cell phone or iPad screen to our eyes is far more damaging than a television on the other side of the room. Lastly, a television show has a consistency in its sound, colors, and characters, and it moves slower than the rapid-fire images our kids are scrolling through on their screens.

Let's think of technology like food—that's something everyone can relate to! If we feed our bodies a steady diet of fast food and junk food, there are consequences: we gain weight, crave sugar, feel sluggish, and can develop a whole host of underlying medical issues. Some of these outcomes are visible, like weight gain, and some, like diabetes, are not. The Standard American Diet (SAD) is less than ideal for optimal nutrition and performance. Alternately, if you eat a diet high in antioxidant-rich fruits and vegetables, high-quality proteins, and healthy fats, your body will show the benefits. It's a dual case of what you *are* doing (eating junk food) and what you're *not* doing (eating healthy food)—both are equally important. If we let our children feast on a diet full of screens and digital devices, we are compromising their long-term health and development.

Parenting in the digital world is a fairly new concept for most parents, since new applications are coming out at lightning speed. Within a very short time frame, people have turned into hamsters on a wheel; swiping, scrolling, liking, and a whole collection of other verbs that didn't even exist ten years ago. I am confident that, deep down, most parents wonder if all this time that kids spend looking down into their screens is really good for them. The science is just starting to become available on this topic, and the results are troublesome to say the least.

My youngest son will be turning sixteen this year, and he's starting to talk about driver's education. He looked at me in shock when I told him one of the most important things about driving is to remember this lesson: a car

> The idea that the brain can be changed by experience is called "plasticity"—the brain is moldable, like plastic.

is a weapon. Every single time you get behind the wheel, you need to be on high alert and not be distracted, because the machine you are controlling could hurt you or someone else. I was sad to have to be so blunt, but I wanted him to understand the magnitude of the responsibility, especially since I know the decision-making frontal lobe of the teen brain hasn't matured yet. Talk about not wanting to drive! Fine with me—the older the better, in my opinion. (Side note: four teen drivers so far at my house, five accidents.)

Parents should give their children the same kind of warnings about cell phone usage that they do about driving. It's becoming clear from studies that using a cell phone has potential side effects similar to taking drugs or gambling. Rapid addiction and deteriorated brain functions are proven consequences of too much use. We question the dangers of high school sports such as football and soccer and make sure our kids wear helmets and pads, get concussion training, etc. We need that same amount of due diligence when it comes to technology. This book is a call to action to change that—no more passive adoption of technology. *We* are raising our children, not Silicon Valley!

First, let's take a look at the human brain to see the impact of all this digital madness. In order to understand why the brain is so incredibly fragile and susceptible to damage from our screens, we must start with the concept of "plasticity."

A Puzzle Waiting to Be Finished

When children are born, their brains are far from being fully developed. The brain comes with possibilities for development, a puzzle waiting to be filled in with stimuli, experiences, and knowledge. The idea that the brain can be changed by experience is called "plasticity"—the brain is moldable, like plastic. The cues and stimuli that are present during brain development really change the way it works later in life. Primary brain development occurs between birth and age twenty-five.[1]

Between birth and age three, our brains develop quickly and are particularly sensitive to the environment around us. In medical circles, this is called the critical period because the changes that happen in the brain during these first tender years become the permanent foundation upon which all later brain function is built. In order for the brain's neural networks to develop normally during the critical period, a child needs specific stimuli from the outside environment.[2]

Think of the studies about babies who grow up in an orphanage without a mother's voice, care, and touch—we now have fifty years of research documenting the side effects of those experiences. Children raised in orphanages can experience structural and functional changes in their brains in terms of IQ, language, speech, and vocabulary. A meta-analysis of seventy-five studies covering over 3,800 children in nineteen countries found an average IQ drop of twenty points. In orphanages throughout Europe, Africa, Asia, and South America, babies have learned not to cry because they realized no one will comfort them. An exposure to silence at a young age can have catastrophic consequences for children's physical and cognitive development.[3]

The brain is literally programmed through our sensory system via the environment in which we grow. The five main sensory systems are taste, sight, touch, smell, and hearing. How many of these essential stimuli are found on our children's screens? Sight and hearing. A toddler can see a picture of a lemon on a screen, or can touch a lemon, smell a lemon, taste a lemon. Learning what an object is from a flat, one-dimensional screen falls far short of the real thing. Tablets are the ultimate shortcut tools. I recently read a good narrative on this topic:

> Unlike a mother reading a story to a child, for example, a smartphone-told story spoon-feeds images, words, and pictures all at once to a young reader. Rather than having to take the time to process a mother's voice into words, visualize complete pictures and exert a mental effort to follow a story line, kids who follow stories on their smartphones get lazy. The device does the thinking for them, and as a result, their own cognitive muscles remain weak.[4]

The brain has four lobes—parietal, temporal, occipital, and frontal—and matures from back to front. The frontal lobes are the least mature during teen years. [5] Connections between the neurons in our brains are what cause us to think the way we do. 80 percent of these connections are formed by what we do prior to age 25.[6]

When children get hooked on tablets and smartphones, they cause real and permanent damage to their fragile, developing brains. "The ability to focus, to concentrate, to lend attention, to sense other people's attitudes and communicate with them, to build a large vocabulary—all those abilities are harmed. And not just for a while. If the damage happens during these crucial early years, its results can affect them forever."[7] Dominic O'Brien, a British mnemonist and author of multiple books on memory, stated, "We're becoming more and more stupid, we don't have to work our brains anymore. Children who learn primarily on screens live in such a literal world, what you see is what you get. Abstract thinking and creative imagination get much more difficult."[8]

I interviewed John Doleman, executive director of the Seeds of Change Corporation, who has seen firsthand the effect cell phones have had on an amazing learning opportunity. The mission of Seeds of Change is to enhance science education for high school students by immersing them in tropical field research in the rain forest of Cost Rica. Since the nonprofit was founded in 2008, Mr. Doleman has seen a dramatic shift in the immersion experience with kids bringing their cell phones. He stated: "When we began this project back in 2008, there were not cell phones in the hands of students, so the immersion in science was total and quite profound in what it did for these students. In 2016, students began arriving with cell phones, seemingly to connect to their friends and families back home. The impact that had on the whole group was simply an entirely diminished experience and in some cases a catastrophe. We have now implemented a policy that no cell phones are allowed, hoping to regain the power that we lost to this cultural shift."

As a society, we can't let children miss out on these amazing opportunities for growth and learning. It is our responsibility to help our children build the best brains possible—let's not outsource this to the engineers and developers at Silicon Valley. Parents can't just sit on the sidelines and let kids' gadgets rewire their brains.

The Pusher is Rarely the Addict

In an interview, Steve Jobs, the famous cofounder of Apple, stated that his own children weren't allowed to use iPads! "Actually, we don't allow the iPad in the home. We think it's too dangerous for them in effect."

In my mid-thirties, I worked in the treasury department at Best Buy, a large consumer electronics company based in Minnesota. Was I ever inspired by the vision and passion of its founder, Dick Schulze! My house was full of products I had purchased with my employee discount: my refrigerator, oven, big screen television, and VCR (now I'm dating myself . . .). In my research for this book, I initially assumed the children of the large tech companies would be the first to embrace all the new technology that comes out—iPhone, Apple watch, iPad, virtual reality goggles . . . I imagined they had bathroom mirrors with built-in computer screens, lights controlled by iPad, touchscreens built into their dinner table, the windshields on their cars vision-activated smartphones. . . . Shockingly, the opposite was true.

In an interview, Steve Jobs, the famous cofounder of Apple, stated that his own children weren't allowed to use iPads! "Actually, we don't allow the iPad in the home. We think it's too dangerous for them in effect." He said this because he recognized just how addictive the iPad is as a vehicle for delivering things to people. "[Once] you had the iPad in front of you, or when you took it away from the home with you, you'd always have access to these platforms that were very addictive. That were hard to resist."[9] In another article, he said, "We limit how much technology our kids use at home."[10] What? I checked to see if he was an anomaly and quickly found many other top Silicon Valley executives and venture capitalists who do not allow their own children to have smartphones or use iPads or computers.

Microsoft Company founder Bill Gates has revealed that he limits his children's exposure to technology. "The world's richest person says his kids clamored for mobile phones as young teenagers, but he and his wife Melinda ignored their complaints until they turned fourteen." He also imposes rules on gadget use in the home, including set times for no screens and no phones on the table during meals.[11]

Evan Williams, a founder of Twitter, refused to give his two sons an iPad but gave them hundreds of books instead.[12]

Alex Constantinople—the CEO of Outcast Agency, a tech-focused communication and marketing firm—said her youngest son, who is five, is never allowed to use gadgets during the week. Her older children, ten to thirteen, are allowed only thirty minutes a day on school nights.[13]

Chris Anderson, the chief executive of the drone maker 3D Robotics, has instituted time limits and parental controls on every device in his home. "My kids accuse me and my wife of being fascists and overly concerned about tech, and they say that none of their friends have the same rules," he said of his five children, ages six to seventeen. "That's because we have seen the dangers of technology firsthand. I've seen it in myself, I don't want to see that happen to my kids."[14] The dangers he is referring to include exposure to harmful content like pornography, bullying from other kids, and—perhaps worst of all—addiction to their devices.

Chamath Palihapitiya, a former Facebook executive and current co-owner of the Golden State Warriors, says he feels tremendous guilt for helping build Facebook into the behemoth it is today. "It literally is at a point now we've created tools that are ripping apart the social fabric of how society works. If you feed the beast, the beast will destroy you." He said he rarely if ever uses Facebook now and added he would not let his own children use it.[15]

Mark Cuban, the billionaire tech entrepreneur and star of ABC's *Shark Tank*, was recently interviewed by CNBC and says he was very strict when it comes to his kids' use of technology. He says it's because he "knows too much." Cuban makes his thirteen-year-old daughter turn in her phone at ten o'clock at night during the week and eleven o'clock on weekends. He also monitors what apps she's using and can shut off her phone activity. "I'm sneaky as can be," he says. "And she hates it."[16]

Most shocking of all, there is even a school in California that doesn't allow the use of any tech—no computers, no iPads, no iPhones. It's called the Waldorf School, and 75 percent of the students are children of Silicon Valley tech executives.[17] This low-tech model is used in all the Waldorf Schools, which currently have 1,000 locations in sixty countries. They slowly integrate technology into the curriculum starting around age fourteen.

It is baffling that these Silicon Valley executives can passionately design, market, and sell their products to us, yet keep them away from their own children. It's the old "Do as I say, not as I do." Could you imagine a personal trainer not letting his own kids work out and stay in shape? Or a nutritionist teaching her patients all about healthy eating, then limiting fruits and vegetables for her own kids and feeding them a steady supply of junk food?

After years of these big technology companies looking away while they post record profits, we are now starting to see former Silicon Valley insiders and whistleblowers going to the media in droves to sound the alarm about what they see as an unregulated and out-of-control industry. One such insider is Tristan Harris, a former Google executive and the current founder of "The Center of Humane Technology." Harris and his world-class team understand how technology hijacks our minds and are advancing thoughtful solutions to change the system. Their objective is to realign technology with humankind's best interest.[18]

It's also not just tech gurus who limit their children's technology. Prince William and Duchess Kate have gone so far as to ban iPads at home: "They're very much seen as Mummy and Daddy's toys, not for children."[19] Simon Cowell said he actually gave up his mobile phone entirely, and feels so much happier as a result.[20] Actress and singer Jennifer Lopez said that in 2015 she instituted a system that only allowed her nine-year-old twins to use tablets and play video games on Sundays.[21] Actor Hugh Jackman also instituted a no-screen rule during the week because he didn't want his kids' downtime to be spent in front of a screen.[22]

These execs and celebrities seem to know something that the rest of us don't. They follow the code of the drug dealer made famous by *Scarface* and the Notorious B.I.G.: never get high on your own supply. This common streetwise jargon implies if you're a drug dealer, don't take the drugs you're dealing, or you'll become addicted yourself. You'll lose your focus, lose sight of your goals, and stop making money.

The tech execs don't let their own children become glued to their devices because they know it can lead to a new phenomenon called *behavioral addiction*. In fact, the primary goal of the design engineers they hire is to get us addicted!

Webster's dictionary defines addiction as a "dependence on or commitment to a habit, practice, or habit-forming substance to the extent that its cessation causes trauma."[23] Today, the majority of smartphone users couldn't go even one day without their cell phones without experiencing trauma! The cell phone has become as vital to our daily existence as the air we breathe. Like our wallet or car keys, we must have it when we leave the house to feel fully dressed and ready to face the day.

For centuries, the big addictions were substances and gambling. That was it. Fast-forward to 2017 and addictions virtually unheard of just a mere decade ago have arrived: social media, binge watching, online porn, email, nonstop work access, video games, smartphones, YouTube videos, activity monitors, and online shopping. All these activities are now readily available 24-7, portable, and can be used behind closed doors. Unlike the chain smokers or heroin addicts of the past, most of today's addicts hide relatively easily. While the age of behavioral addiction is still in its infancy in the United States, all signs point to an inevitable crisis. We need only look at South Korea and China, who are years ahead of the United States in technology adoption—more on that topic later in this chapter.

Dopamine (The Happy Hormone)

> Research on video games shows dopamine is released during gaming, and cravings for video games produce brain changes that are similar to drug cravings.

We can't go any further discussing addiction without a brief discussion of dopamine. Memorize that word and teach it to your older kids: those eight little letters can wreak havoc on your child's brain development and mental health.

Dopamine is a molecule in our brains that aids in the creation of desire and pleasure—thus its nickname, the "happy hormone." This chemical drives professional football and basketball players, Broadway performers, and concert pianists to put in years of practice to achieve their dreams. But it's also the force that fuels drug addiction. When people use drugs, their dopamine levels spike, and as a result they feel an instant flush of pleasure. But while they initially feel euphoria with just a small amount, their bodies build up a tolerance so that each time they require a little more to get that same initial feeling. Technically, their brains actually think the chemical release is an error, so with each hit of the drug the brain produces less and less dopamine. The same holds true for your kids and their devices. More time with technology is required to produce the same initial response. This is what makes your child's devices so dangerous; think of it as digital heroin. "The risk is, if unchecked, a child could pursue that digital high again and again, until it becomes an unhealthy habit that literally impacts their brain function."[24]

Over time, the dopamine receptors and transporters become sluggish and reduce in number. Research on video games shows dopamine is released during gaming, and cravings for video games produce brain changes that are similar to drug cravings. Dr. Aric Sigman warns about constant dopamine release in young minds: "There are concerns among neuroscientists that this dopamine being produced every single day for many years—through, for example, playing computer games—may change the reward circuitry in a child's brain and make them more dependent [on] onscreen media."[25]

> Children who develop addictions to screens are much more susceptible to developing other addictions someday. Research suggests 90 percent of addictions have roots in the teen years.

More dopamine is present during the teen years than the rest of your life. Adolescent hormone levels intensify a good or a bad feeling. "When a child even thinks about his Twitter account or Snapchat, dopamine stimulates the reward centers of the brain to seek it. If she makes a habit of going on Snapchat at homework time, she'll condition herself to its attention-grabbing level of stimulation. She'll lose patience for less stimulating activities like answering review questions."[26]

As another pretty clear example of the high dopamine levels, I want to briefly touch on the "E-Word" recently used by the United States Surgeon General. After back-to-back reports came out discussing skyrocketing rates of teen e-cigarette use, the Surgeon General, in December 2018, declared youth vaping an EPIDEMIC. Fueled by Juul's USB-shaped products, a whopping 78 percent increase in vaping among high school students was reported by the FDA and CDC in just one year![27]

These increases are unprecedented and shocking to say the least. This is just my opinion, but could the rapid penetration of smart phone usage among teens and now the epidemic size vaping somehow be linked? There is evidence to support teens being much more susceptible to addiction, which I will talk about in the next paragraph.

Most likely, it will take years before scientific studies are completed on the addictive qualities of vapes, but even a rudimentary understanding of addiction shows how important it is to keep these products away from children. Parents, if you've read this, consider yourself warned. Off my soap box, on to the data . . .

The National Center on Addiction and Substance Abuse at Columbia University tells us why addiction is more prevalent during formative years than it is during adulthood: "Because the teen brain is still developing, addictive substances physically alter its structure and function faster and more intensely than in adults, interfering with brain development, further impairing judgment and heightening the risk of addiction. Children who develop addictions to screens are much more susceptible to developing other addictions someday. Research suggests 90 percent of addictions have roots in the teen years. To further drive home this point, one in four Americans who began using any addictive substance before age eighteen are addicted, compared to one in twenty-five who started using at age twenty-one or older."[28] Read that again. Repeat. Read that again. Repeat.

It's important to note that researchers generally agree there's a latency period of about ten years or more before the damage shows up—so you may not be seeing the symptoms in your children right now, but they are hidden deep within the brain.

Lucky for those of us in the United States, we don't have to wait years to see what this technology addiction is going to do to our children. All we have to do is look at those countries that were early adopters of all the new technologies and where they are now. Let's drill down to a couple big ones: China and South Korea.

Gaming and internet addiction is a serious problem throughout East Asia. In China, there are millions of youngsters with this problem, and the country actually has camps where parents commit their children for months in hopes of a cure. South Korea has one of the world's greatest populations of internet users, with 93 percent having access to the internet. It also boasts a high percentage of smartphone users: 72 percent of South Korean children now own their first smartphone by the time they turn twelve. In fact, 88 percent of adults own a smartphone.[29]

Technology addiction is such a problem in these two countries that there are proposals for something they call Cinderella Laws. The idea is to protect children from playing certain games after midnight.[30] The government is proposing a ban on children under eighteen playing video games between midnight and eight in the morning. "A draft law would make it compulsory for computers and smartphones to be fitted with software that would track young night owls who flout the gaming ban."[31]

If you go to some big cities in the United States, you can find separate transportation lanes for bike riders. These lanes have proven to be a great way to facilitate and promote exercise and a healthy lifestyle. On the other hand, some places in China now have separate lanes for those walking while using their cell phone. They're called "Distracted Walker Lanes"—the first mobile phone sidewalks. Inattentive walkers have caused so many accidents that they now get their own lane.

Digital addiction is so rampant that treatment centers are popping up all over the world. China alone has three hundred treatment facilities. South Korea has over two hundred government-sponsored counseling programs. Japan has summer camps called "fasting camps" where kids go cold turkey with no technology. The United States only has four residential treatment programs for internet addiction: the reSTART-gaming addiction center in Washington, the Internet Addiction Treatment Recovery Program in Pennsylvania, the Illinois Institute for Addiction, and the Center for Internet and Technology Addiction in Connecticut. These programs are very costly—for example, reSTART is $25,000 for the first month and $8,500 per month for outpatient care. The others range from $3,000 to $45,000 per month.[32]

Why the disparity in numbers of treatment programs? It can't be population, since South Korea has 51 million people and the United States has 323 million. The United States is just late to the party, which is not surprising, as our healthcare is largely driven by insurance and health regulations. Some other countries have officially recognized tech addiction as a disorder, which has helped lead their governments and healthcare providers to develop initiatives to control the problem.

A shift is starting, however, as two new government studies have recently been announced. For the first time in the United States, a two-year study on internet addiction is being funded by the National Institute of Health (NIH) and kicked off in August 2017. This may ultimately help to determine whether addiction to online gaming should be listed in the *Diagnostic and Statistical Manual of Mental Disorders.*[33] This could dramatically change insurance coverage for teens at risk for addiction.

But more importantly, in December 2018, the United States federal government, through the National Institute of Health, announced on *60 Minutes* the most ambitious study of adolescent brain development ever attempted. It is trying to understand what screens are doing to children's brains, emotional development, and mental health. At twenty-one sites across the country, scientists have begun interviewing nine and ten year olds and scanning their brains. They'll follow more than 11,000 kids for ten years and spend $300 million![34]

The interviews and data from the first wave of 4,500 kids who participated in this study have just been released. Shockingly, the results showed that kids who spend more than two hours a day on screens got lower scores on thinking and language tests.[35] TWO HOURS!

Smokes and Slots

Once you understand the role dopamine plays in addiction, it's not a big surprise there is a worldwide tech addiction problem. There are thousands of people trained in brain neurology and addiction habits whose sole job is to get you hooked. They work at Apple, Google, Samsung, Yahoo, Facebook, and Netflix. They want you to pick up that phone or device all day long! Never before in history have a handful of people and a handful of companies shaped how a billion people think and feel every day with the choices they make on their screens.[36] By their very design, cell phones are made to get us addicted. In fact, their whole business defines success around "time spent" or repeat sessions. Other than drugs, I can think of only two products in the history of the world that have had similarly addictive tendencies: cigarettes and slot machines.

A good friend of mine is an educator who has taught for over twenty-five years at the second largest high school in Minnesota. She cleverly refers to her students' phones as "smokes" and regularly says, "Put your smokes away now!" I firmly believe that technology will follow a similar trajectory to cigarettes, and right now we are in the Marlboro Man stage. How can we forget the glamor and allure of the rugged Marlboro cowboy on all the billboards and commercials?

> Computer programmers understand the reward centers of our brains, and they know how to juice their apps to make them addictive. They call it "brain hacking"—feeling the need to check your phone often.

Men, women, and children were drawn to him, and cigarette sales skyrocketed after that campaign was launched. The famous icon of the global cigarette and tobacco company Philip Morris was a legend from the mid-1950s all the way to 1999. And let's not forget how cool Marlon Brando made smoking in *A Streetcar Named Desire*—or, for that matter, Humphrey Bogart in *Casablanca*, the glamorous Audrey Hepburn in *Breakfast at Tiffany's*, and John Travolta in *Grease*.

Ironically, at least four of the actors who portrayed the Marlboro man have died of smoking-related diseases. A hundred and fifty years after Philip Morris launched their first cigarette in 1847, a massive tobacco lawsuit was settled, and the big four tobacco companies agreed to put cancer warnings on cigarettes, discontinue advertising to youth, and follow a host of other severe penalties meant to inform everyone of the dangers of tobacco. I would love it if the tech monopolies were forced to pay for social media, television, and billboard advertising showing parents and teens how addictive their products can become if used excessively. Maybe after the NIH study is completed in the summer of 2019, we can get a "black box" warning on all new cell phones, similar to the surgeon general's warning on cigarette packs.

Tobacco isn't the only addiction that is similar to screen use—how about gambling's easy favorite, the slot machine? Las Vegas, Nevada, is full of slot machines, penny slots, quarter slots, dollar slots . . . when you pull a lever, sometimes you get nothing and sometimes you get a reward in points or cash. This concept is called "intermittent variable reward." It's unpredictable, exciting, and addicting. The engineers who design your phone use the same logic to get you hooked. When you pick up your phone, you sometimes—but not always—get a reward in the form of likes on Facebook and Instagram, new followers on Twitter, friend requests, or even flirty emojis in a text message.

Computer programmers understand the reward centers of our brains, and they know how to juice their apps to make them addictive. They call it "brain hacking"—feeling the need to check your phone often. Silicon Valley is engineering your phone and social media to get you hooked.[37] For example—sometimes, instead of doling out "likes" as they come in, app designers will hold them back and then deliver them later in a burst. The exact timing and size of the burst is calculated and perfected to each individual user.

If you put someone in front of a slot machine, their brain will look qualitatively the same as when they take heroin. If you're someone who compulsively plays video games, the minute you load up your computer your brain will look like that of a substance abuser. "The people who are making the games are designing them to hook us, to get us addicted, to make it so we don't want to do anything else," according to Dr. David Rosenberg.[38]

In order to comprehend the business side of this digital landscape, I want to briefly touch on what I see as the motivation for these large monopolies. Let's use one example, Facebook. We shouldn't be naïve enough to think that the engineers and executives at Facebook are strategically trying to figure out how to get Suzie Homemaker more friends on Facebook so that she's happier. No, their goal is to get Suzie's eyeballs looking at their content and their advertisers. To succeed as a business, they must figure out how to monetize Suzie's time, clicks, and swipes online. The address of Facebook headquarters at "1 Hacker Way" epitomizes the company's motto of "move fast and break things."

Facebook uses extremely complicated algorithms to follow Suzie's digital trail on her phone, iPad, and computer, and uses her browsing history to market specifically to her tastes. It's the world's largest and most invasive surveillance network, where they capture, record, and retain what each individual user is doing. That's why Facebook doesn't cost any money: someone is paying them to get your attention so you can buy products and services. But Facebook is not free; we pay by submitting ourselves to their surveillance. The personal data they collect on users is their most valuable asset, which is why their initial public offering in 2012 was valued at $100 billion!

Google is another example of the large cost we pay to have constant connectivity by allowing unprecedented invasions of our privacy. They currently have a monopoly on several markets, including search engines and advertising. Bing, their closest web search competitor, has just 2 percent of the market; Google has 90 percent. Google controls 60 percent of the global advertising revenue on the internet, and catches every single thing you do online when using a Google-based feature to build powerful personality profiles of all users. That includes Gmail, Google search, Google Docs, and Chrome.[39]

All these engineering strategies to keep us coming back are wreaking havoc on our physical and mental health.

Pornography, the Poisonous Pictures

No discussion of screen addiction is complete without a look at the often-secondary addiction of pornography. I am definitely taking one for the team writing on this subject. I'm blushing and embarrassed, but I must rise above my discomfort to help save our children from one of the biggest threats to their ability to have lasting and loving relationships in the future.

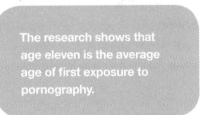

The research shows that age eleven is the average age of first exposure to pornography.

I know this is a subject no one likes to talk about. We all want to think we can keep our kids pure and innocent well into their adolescent years. Like many parents, I am scared my son's sheltered childhood will come to an abrupt end when he accidentally stumbles on pornography. Once those nude pictures are seen, I know they will forever be branded on his memory. But the reality is that in this age of connectivity, it's not a matter of *if* your children will be exposed to pornography; it's a matter of *when*. The research shows that age eleven is the average age of first exposure to pornography.[40] We can't bury our heads in the sand and hope this risk goes away, or that our child will be one of the lucky ones spared the dark side of the internet. The statistics on childhood porn use are disturbing, and it's up to us as parents to turn the tide in our own homes.

When I was growing up, if a neighborhood boy somehow snagged himself a *Playboy* or *Penthouse* magazine, he was the most popular kid on the block—it was like he'd won the golden ticket. (Of course, that's the recollection of a naïve little Catholic-school girl; who knows, maybe every teen boy out there knew where the secret stash was.) Adult movies that showed sexuality comparable to the online videos available today

> Think triple A's, folks: porn is *affordable*, it's *accessible*, and most of all, it's *anonymous*.

were rated "R" and could not be seen without ID, eliminating that as an option for curious teens. (There were the famous three- to five-second nudity flashes boys drooled over in *Airplane!* and *Sixteen Candles*.) You might find the occasional willing participant to go in the barn or behind the shed with you, but that too was rare. Now, the pictures that live in our kids' pockets are ready to be set free like a genie from a lamp with one quick swipe of a screen.

So why is porn so easily accessible online? Aren't there laws to protect our children from all the smut? Yes, and no. The federal obscenity laws do make it illegal to distribute hardcore porn, but there is no specific government agency set up to enforce the laws, making it essentially up to the local prosecutor's discretion. Based upon the number of adult peep stores out there and the endless supply of porn videos on the internet, it appears the DA's office is busy with other criminals. As for softcore porn (think nude photographs), I couldn't find any laws against that. I guess a static picture may not be as damaging as a motion picture, but depending on the age of the child, trauma could clearly occur with still nudes. Is this explosion of porn really just symbolic of the moral relativism so prevalent in today's society, where everybody can just decide for themselves what's right and what's wrong?

Once again, as with the magnet that pulls our kids to their screens, at the heart of this filth's proliferation is an industry whose bread and butter is dependent on people watching and buying their smut. They make money when people show up to drool over degrading and aggressive sexual acts demonstrated by paid actors and actresses, many of whom are underage. When our children view pornography, they are unintentionally perpetuating the whole porn industry.

So how did we go from a few *Playboy* magazines stashed under a teen's mattress to hardcore porn available 24-7? Think triple A's, folks: porn is *affordable* (nearly every household has an internet connection), it's *accessible* (on your phone, tablet, and laptop and in your bedroom, bathroom, and basement), and most of all, it's *anonymous*. Before, only the mailman and nosy neighbors knew who had the magazine delivered in the brown-paper wrapper. Today, no one will ever find out if your son or daughter is in their room watching hardcore porn when you think they're watching an episode of *Modern Family*. (Don't lose heart—the right software can block most of this, which I will discuss in Solution 50)

Since I'm a CPA, my first inclination is usually "Show me the numbers," so let's take a look at the statistics and see how big a problem this is for our kids. About twenty years ago, the US Department of Justice stated, "Never before in the history of telecommunications media in the United States has so much indecent (and obscene) material been so easily accessible by so many minors in so many American homes with so few restrictions." Remarkably, this was said before the iPhone, before the advent of 4G networks, and before the term "Wi-Fi" was even trademarked. Only a few years after the invention of the web browser, porn had become a noted problem among young people.[41]

A shocking "79 percent of youth's unwanted exposure to porn occurs in the home."

Clearly, the internet was the impetus for the rapid explosion in porn accessibility—so what did its more sophisticated offspring, the smartphone, do for the porn industry? "In April 2016 the Barna Group completed the largest study ever completed on pornography called 'The Porn

Phenomenon.' The data concluded that 93 percent of boys and 62 percent of girls have been exposed to pornography before the age of eighteen. In addition, 64 percent of thirteen to twenty-four-year-olds seek out porn weekly."[42] I can't even imagine what is going to happen when virtual-reality technology brings porn to a whole new level; it's downright creepy.

If you're curious where our current high schoolers are heading, a good starting point would be the slightly older millennials, since they were the first generation to grow up with internet in their homes, but before smartphones. Today, "79% of men in that generation say they watch pornography at least once a month (and most of these watch porn several times a week); 64% of women say they watch porn at least once a month."[43]

And even more troubling is that porn use is occurring right under our noses. A shocking "79 percent of youth's unwanted exposure to porn occurs in the home."[44] In fact, many kids are accidentally stumbling on this while doing their homework. Children's character names like Pokémon and Action Man are linked to thousands of porn links.[45]

To make matters worse, today's youth are not only watching porn, they are *becoming* porn! The practice of "sexting" is rampant in today's teen culture. Our kids are sending an endless number of explicit text messages, provocative bikini pictures, or even full-blown nude images or videos (referred to as "nudes"). They often think they can just send it on Snapchat and it will disappear, but those images can be preserved for eternity. Angry ex-boyfriends are posting sexual images of their former girlfriends online, a practice often nicknamed "revenge porn." What often follows is cyberbullying by classmates, where girls are shamed for participating in something they most likely thought was love.

I recently sat down with a mother who discussed this exact issue. The mom discovered that an eighth-grade boy was sending pornographic photos to her fourteen-year-old daughter, asking if she would "do this or that to him." The daughter was deleting the photos before the parents could see what was going on, but luckily the images were caught on one of their monitoring applications. Their daughter made a good choice and did not succumb to the boy's pressure, and her parents could guide her through the perils of sexting. Not all stories end that well.

It's really no surprise this is happening when you consider the sexual images kids are exposed to by today's mass media. Magazine covers, advertisements, music videos, fashion styles, and even Barbie dolls celebrate sex appeal. Take a look at the sexuality displayed in some of the video games your kids are playing, like *Grand Theft Auto*—images like that subtly alter the way men view women.

I think, instinctually, we all know pornography is not healthy for our children, but why, specifically, is it damaging? To me, the danger of pornography is the impact it has on our children physically, psychologically, and relationally. Since I am a Catholic, I think a fourth side effect of porn use is damage to your spirituality, since it takes you away from a deep and intimate relationship with God. Truthfully, any time you have a secret that you hide from loved ones, the whole relationship suffers, as do you.

The number-one physical effect of pornography is addiction. Repeated viewing triggers dopamine receptors, just like the other substance addictions discussed earlier in this chapter. In a certain way, pornography addiction can be even worse than substance abuse. At least with drugs or alcohol, the body can get rid of the substance over a few days. But once your child views shocking pictures, they will be in their memory forever. With each viewing of porn, the child needs more and more exposure to have that same initial pleasure. It's like they got a little taste of crack and want more. C.S. Lewis describes this law of diminishing returns in *The Screwtape Letters*: "An ever-increasing craving for an ever-diminishing pleasure."

Extended use of porn can quickly morph into a full-blown sex addiction. Sex addiction can come in many forms, especially as teens mature into adulthood. Major types of acting out include excessive viewing of pornography, compulsive masturbation, use of prostitutes, hookups, and extramarital affairs. When we chase this artificial euphoria as adults, the consequences are painful. Pornography can be the gateway to adultery, since the infidelity starts in your head—imagining yourself with the person on the screen, not your spouse as God intended. There's a reason two of the Ten Commandments cover adultery! We need to stop this porn viewing in its tracks to avoid setting our kids up for these adult problems, which can destroy any intimate and loving relationships they may want to pursue.

Pornography is also particularly damaging to a child given the immature development of the brain. As a pediatrician for over thirty years and a consultant for the National Center for Missing and Exploited Children, Dr. Sharon Cooper has seen the devastating impact pornography can have on the mind

> Porn promises what it cannot deliver: fulfillment of the human need for connection and intimacy.

of a child. She explains that pornography is neurologically more damaging to a child than to an adult for at least two reasons.

Children have an abundance of "mirror neurons" in their brains. Mirror neurons convince us that, when we see something, we are actually experiencing it. If you've ever been watching a sporting event where someone suddenly gets clobbered in the face with a ball, your body might automatically recoil as if you were the one who was hit: that's your mirror neurons ringing. When a man watches pornography, his mirror neurons activate, eventually triggering an erection because his body now believes it is experiencing sex. Researchers believe the abundance of mirror neurons in children makes pornography "more real" to them.

Children also have an immature prefrontal cortex. This is the area of the brain that controls judgment, controls impulses, and regulates emotion. This region of the brain isn't mature until between ages twenty to twenty-two. Because children have such a weak prefrontal cortex, they lack the "executive control" to stop the flow of emotions and sensations that come from watching porn.[46] Porn has also been proven to actually shrink the prefrontal cortex![47] Another physical symptom caused by long-term porn use is erectile dysfunction. This is not the fairly common vascular problem of ED, but a side effect caused by repeated exposure to pornography and masturbation.

The psychological effects of pornography include shame, guilt, trauma, depression, anxiety, and loss of confidence.[48] This is understandable; although you can hide your fantasy life behind closed doors, you can't hide it from yourself. That moral compass is in there for a reason: to guide our behaviors. There's tremendous guilt and shame in living with the secrets and deceit that go along with hiding a porn problem. When children use porn, we shouldn't shame them or make them feel bad. These desires are kicked off by a natural curiosity. We do, however, need to intervene early and redirect them to more positive and constructive thoughts and activities. We cannot allow their curiosity to dive into this dangerous world which can all too often enslave the visitor.

When adults use porn, it's not driven by innocent curiosity; it's to self-medicate, to feel accepted, to avoid feelings of abandonment, or to dull their emotions. The porn is just masking the underlying problems, most of which are normal life challenges. Porn promises what it cannot deliver: fulfillment of the human need for connection and intimacy. As with AA, there is a twelve-step program for adults with sexual addiction that has proven very helpful in freeing the addict. Let's hope our children never get to that level!

Beyond the psychological and physical ramifications of porn use, there is a huge impact to society as a whole and relationally between couples when we have a generation of kids getting their sex education from a screen. The most important flaw in this practice is that kids are getting a warped sense of what a real, deep, intimate, and loving relationship looks like. Most real women do not look like porn stars, nor do they engage in the brutal and often degrading sexual acts depicted in porn videos. It's interesting to me that watching porn can make a man "feel like a real man" without requiring him to actually be one. There's nothing "real" about it. Real men don't lust after inanimate and anonymous women on their screen. Real men love the people in their life deeply and give of themselves selflessly to build a real human connection. As a teen named Wade told Minnesota Public Radio, "Pornography is hot sex and cold emotion."[49] Does that sound like the relationship model we want our children exposed to? No, we need our teen boys to know that the woman who is coming to deliver the pizza is just the woman here to deliver the pizza.

Beyond the mere threat to real relationships, the porn industry objectifies women who are often runaways or part of a larger sex trafficking ring. It also makes young men think that violence in sexual activity is acceptable and that women are to be subjugated. Sexual activity in the context of a loving relationships is so much more than sexual arousal and pleasure. According to Jean Twenge, author of *iGen*, "These are not videos of two people who love each other having hot sex—they are actors who participate in sex that is often brutal and almost always emotionally distant. Pornography does not portray normal adult sexuality. As a result, a generation of teens is getting a warped view of what sex is about; according to most pornography, it's about the man's pleasure only, often at the woman's expense."[50]

I know this is all hard data to take in, especially if you have kids who are acting on their curiosity. Don't lose hope; in my final chapter, I will give a great solution to get you started on the difficult topic of pornography with your children. We are not alone in this battle. With our guidance and God's grace, they can fight the darkness that lives in this underground world of pornography.

The Anxiety Society

SWIPE. SCROLL. SURF. BINGE. FORWARD.
SNAP. CLICK. TEXT. LIKE. LOVE. TWEET.
RETWEET. POST. CHARGE. FRIEND.
COMMENT. SHARE. KIK.

I'm getting anxious just typing all the things our kids do on their devices . . . the devices we have purchased and continue to pay for. While our intentions are good, these screens are having serious negative effects on their mental health and happiness. "It's not an exaggeration to describe this new iGen as being on the brink of the worst mental-health crisis in decades."[51] We live in a world where even the POTUS's preferred mode of communication is the middle-of-the-night tweet. Some of the mental-health side effects of too much screen time are staggering and include:

ANXIETY STRESS DEPRESSION FATIGUE
LONELINESS SELF-HARM NOMOPHOBIA
INSECURTY PHANTOM VIBRATION SYNDROME

Listed below are just a few of the studies available on the skyrocketing rates of mental health problems we are now facing—more data is being released weekly. I know these are just numbers on a page, but the implications are staggering for the health and happiness of our children. Please read through each study slowly so the magnitude of the problem really sinks in.

- Recent research shows anxiety—characterized by constant and overwhelming worry and fear—is now 800 percent more prevalent than all forms of cancer.[52]

- 38 percent of girls ages thirteen to seventeen, and 26 percent of boys the same age, have an anxiety disorder.[53] If you have a teenage girl, that means almost four out of ten of her friends have anxiety! And for boys, it's one out of four, so sad.

- More than half of all American college students suffer from anxiety. Meanwhile, the number of web searches involving the term has nearly doubled over the last five years.[54]

- Data from the National Institute of Mental Health (NIMH) suggests the prevalence of people with anxiety disorders in the US may be as high as forty million—about 18 percent of the population over the age of eighteen—making it the most common mental illness in the nation.[55]

- "Suicide is the third-leading cause of death in Americans between the ages of ten and twenty-four. Teens who spend three hours a day or more on electronic devices are 35 percent more likely to have a risk factor for suicide, such as making a suicide plan."[56]

- More than half of UK cell phone users suffer from "nomophobia"—no-mobile-phone phobia—and the number may be even higher for American users.[57]

- If you've ever felt your phone vibrating in your pocket, pulled it out, and realized it wasn't ringing, you've experience "phantom vibration syndrome" and according to researchers at

"It's not an exaggeration to describe this new iGen as being on the brink of the worst mental-health crisis in decades."

the University of Michigan Institute for Social Research, it's a sign of addiction. When people have addictions, there's a phenomenon in which they are hypersensitive to sensations associated with a rewarding stimulus.[58]

It's easy to understand how we can fall prey to the hallucinations of phantom vibration syndrome, since many people carry their phone in their pocket and it seems part of their body. I guess you could compare it to how I wear my eyeglasses—they are clearly always on my face and are like a body part since I wouldn't see well without them. However, I never expect my eyeglasses to do anything, so I'm not on high alert waiting for the next "reward" to come in. We need to get these gadgets out of our pockets.

Mark Zuckerberg, the famous founder of Facebook, has been quoted as saying the mission of Facebook is "To give people the power to share and make the world more open and connected."[59] I'm sorry to burst your bubble, Mr. Zuckerberg, but your platform is not necessarily making people feel connected, as rates of loneliness continue to escalate; the price of this connectivity is all too often anxiety and depression, not to mention constant surveillance.

- "Facebook may be more harmful than helpful to your emotional well-being, raising your risk of depression—especially if your contacts' posts elicit envy."[60]

- "In a month-long experiment at the University of Pennsylvania, college students who limited themselves to just 30 minutes a day on Facebook, Instagram, and Snapchat reported significant decrease in loneliness and depression."[61]

- A recent report from the Royal Society of Public Health (RSPH) and the Young Health Movement examined the influence Facebook and other social media sites have on young people's mental health, and the analysis didn't reflect well on most social networks. "Of the five major platforms analyzed, only YouTube was found to have a positive impact on users. According to the report's survey, the other four (Facebook, Instagram, Snapchat, and Twitter) increased respondents' feelings of anxiety. Instagram was the most anxiety-inducing, followed by Snapchat."[62]

- "Social media, and Facebook in particular, has long been associated with depression. In 2015 a study from Denmark's Happiness Research Institute claimed that people who stopped using Facebook for a week were happier at the end of their break than those who used it as normal."[63]

Have you ever heard of the "blue zones"? These are the five areas of the world with the oldest and healthiest populations, with many people's age surpassing one hundred years. The biggest contributor to this longevity is their sense of community and belonging. In fact, being isolated socially is a bigger driver of mortality than smoking and drinking.

- Two recent meta-analyses reveal that loneliness is more hazardous to your health than obesity, raising your risk of early death by as much as 50 percent, and compares to the risk of smoking 15 cigarettes per day.[64]

- The number of Americans who say they have no close friends has roughly tripled in recent decades. "A large proportion of the lonely are young; almost two-thirds of sixteen- to twenty-four-year-olds in Britain said they feel lonely at least some of the time, while almost a third are lonely often or all the time."[65]

Let's take a look at how all this swiping and scrolling is affecting our biochemistry and contributing to the mental health crisis.

Cortisol ("The Stress Hormone")

Anxiety caused by wanting to touch, scroll, swipe, and post on our cell phones is easy to understand once you have a grasp of cortisol.

As with the previous eight-letter word we discussed, dopamine, commit this to memory and teach it to your children. Cortisol is a hormone produced by the adrenal gland. It's served a very important evolutionary function, as it puts humans on high alert when danger is present (i.e. the fight or flight response). Kind of like when you're on a leisurely walk and a snake appears right in front of you. Sadly, our adrenal glands have been hacked, and now just putting our phones down can send the same signal as an encounter with a snake in our path. Your phone wants one thing, and that's YOUR ATTENTION! The fastest way to get rid of that anxious feeling is to touch your phone, and then you're stuck a constant loop of touch, wait to touch, touch, wait to touch, touch, have to touch, HAVE to touch, HAVE TO touch, HAVE TO TOUCH . . .

> "Our phones are keeping us in a continual state of anxiety in which the only antidote is the phone."

Larry Rosen, a psychologist at CA State University, conducted research on the effect technology has on our anxiety levels. His results showed that "a typical person checks their phone every fifteen minutes or less, and half the time there is no alert, no new notification. It's a signal coming from inside their head feeling like, hah, I haven't checked Facebook in awhile."[66] The only way to get rid of this anxiety is? Yep, check your phone.

On the television show *20/20* Anderson Cooper did an episode on "Brain Hacking." He was hooked up to monitors to track his heart rate and perspiration. A woman sent text messages to his phone, which was just out of his reach. Every time a text notice beep went off, a blue line spiked on the monitor, indicating anxiety caused by the release of cortisol. "Our phones are keeping us in a continual state of anxiety in which the only antidote is the phone."[67]

On an October 2018 episode of the CNN documentary series *This Is Life with Lisa Ling*, Ms. Ling participated in a similar experiment at Neurospace Labs in Silicon Valley. While the reporter felt very in control and focused during the experiment, the results showed a clear and prominent stress response caused by dividing her attention between the computer task at hand and her chirping cell phone.[68]

Have you ever had a weekend of pure indulgence on caffeine, unhealthy carbs, and sugar? Try to get off that Monday morning, and within a short timeframe comes a headache and sluggishness. Eat a donut and poof, problem solved. However, you're just feeding your sugar addiction and making the problem worse in the long run. Sugar and cell phones—they are this generation's crack cocaine.

Digital Dementia

An alarming, newly diagnosed condition has shaken the medical and research communities. It has been appropriately named "digital dementia." Yes, the same thing that sadly caused Grandma to forget your name is now affecting teens around the world. It is early onset dementia, or a deterioration of cognitive abilities caused by excessive screen time.

> Initial research is attributing the early onset of teen dementia to a lopsided development of the brain caused by excessive device use.

Manfred Spitzer, one of the most famous neuroscientists in Germany, coined the term "digital dementia" in a book of the same name that discusses the adverse effects of internet use on our brains. While he may have been the first to name this phenomenon, he certainly doesn't take credit for being the first to discover it. The condition was originally diagnosed by doctors from South Korea.

Some South Korean teens are presenting memory problems, attention disorders, and emotional flattening caused by spending too much time on the web searching, texting, and viewing multimedia. Those tech-addicted teens showed the same symptoms as dementia patients. Doctors say young people are at particular risk because their brains are still developing.[69] The situation in South Korea is so extreme they even tried a nationwide campaign called "One, One, One." They encouraged kids to stay off their devices one day, once a week, for one hour![70] It's hard to imagine it could get that bad, but if we don't intervene now, the United States could head down that same path.

Initial research is attributing the early onset of teen dementia to a lopsided development of the brain caused by excessive device use. According to Dr. Byun Gi-won, a medical doctor who runs the Balance Brain Center in Seoul, "Overuse of smartphones and game devices hampers the balanced development of the brain. Heavy users are likely to develop the left side of their brains, leaving the right side untapped or underdeveloped."[71] Doctor Kim Youn-bo at Gachon University Gil Medical Center in Incheon notes, "Left-brain skills include rational, linear, fact-finding thinking processes, whereas right-brain skills include intuition, imagination, and emotional thoughts. Since smartphone use mostly stimulates the left side of the brain, the right side, which is linked with concentration, eventually degenerates, reducing attention and memory span." This potentially leads to an early onset of dementia in up to 15 percent of cases.[72]

And loss of our ability to focus is not just a problem for the future: a study from Microsoft suggests that the average human attention span is now only eight seconds, a full second shorter than the nine-second attention span of a goldfish.[73]

"In one study, participants were asked to remember trivia facts as well as which of five corresponding folders the answers were stored in. Interestingly, the participants were able to remember the folder locations better than the actual facts themselves. It seems that instead of storing knowledge, we are now more likely to store the 'how' and 'where' of getting to it. In practical application, we see this every day. A majority of people no longer memorize phone numbers because all they have to do is push a button and dial. Students no longer have to take notes in class: they just snap a picture of the notes on the whiteboard with their smartphones."[74] It's a familiar concept: "Use it or lose it."

A science research paper coming out of a Harvard and Columbia study concluded: "If I use Google to research something, I forget that. Your brain thinks you don't have to remember that because you can always Google that. Little incentive to memorize."[75]

Blue light and high cortisol levels cause amyloid plaque to build up in the brain—one of the hallmarks of Alzheimer's. Katie Couric's podcast discussed a doctor who says he's seeing higher levels of plaque in kids who are using screens, caused by the blue light and high cortisol levels. He said, "The thought of people having memory problems in their 30s and 40s is pretty frightening."[76]

Dr. Spitzer likes to call the aging of our brains "graceful degradation," as opposed to crashing. Your brain can lose a small amount of neurons without you noticing, but when you lose a large portion, you will show symptoms of dementia. The more knowledge you have, the slower the mental decline.[77] Sounds like a great argument for lifelong learning!

The Proof Is in the MRI

The effect screens have on our brains can be hard to imagine—but, now, we have pictures to prove it. Numerous studies have used magnetic resonance imaging (MRI) to view the brains of children who use screens. The evidence is terrifying because big changes have been taking place for years, but we haven't been able to see them until recently.

A brain hooked on the internet, phones, or tablets looks like a brain hooked on heroin.

First, let's start in the lab with mice. In a study conducted at the Center for Brain Research in Seattle Children's Hospital, young mice were exposed to switching sounds and light, similar to what happens when you scroll on your phone or iPad. Your brain is actually trying to multitask by switching back and forth—the researchers wanted to know if the brain functions as well after exposure. Their conclusion: "No, the ability to learn new things was compromised and it took the young mice three times longer to complete simple tasks as did the mice not exposed to switching sounds and lights . . . What's worse, the damage was permanent changes in the brain as illustrated on the MRIs."[78] I will explore this topic in much greater detail in my chapter on multitasking.

I took a road trip to a northern Minnesota high school to watch a private screening of a new documentary titled *Screenagers*. The movie was eye-opening to most of the parents in the room, and I really feel every parent would benefit from seeing it. It was written and produced by pediatrician and mother Dr. Delaney Ruston; she was seeing signs of change in both her teen patients and her own children, and she wanted to figure out what all this new technology was really doing to our kids. In an interview, she stated, "Many studies that look at MRI scans of the brains of kids who play a lot of video games (20 hours or more per week) and when they compared them to people who are addicted to drugs and alcohol, their brain scans are similar."[79]

"Psychiatrist Dr. David Rosenberg showed us MRI images of the brains of children with internet addiction. You can see activity in the brain decrease. 'The brain shuts down and its executive functioning is not working,' said Dr. Rosenberg. He says a brain hooked on the internet, phones, or tablets looks like a brain hooked on heroin."[80] I studied the MRI images and there are clear red areas on the images which point to abnormal white matter in addicted teens.

In a comprehensive summary by Dr. Victoria Dunckley that was published in *Psychology Today*, *M.D.*, neuroimagery was examined to show

how excessive screen time affects the brain. She used the findings of several researchers to explain how the various parts of the brain were changed. Here is a brief summary of all the brain areas negatively affected:[81]

- Atrophy (shrinkage or loss of tissue volume) in gray matter areas; gray matter areas are where processing occurs

- Atrophy in frontal lobe (controls executive functions like planning and organizing)

- Volume loss in striatum (reward pathways)

- Damage to insula (capacity for empathy and compassion)

- Compromised white matter (loss of communication between two sides of the brain)

- Reduced cortical thickness (outermost part of the brain)

- Impaired cognitive function (less efficient, reduced impulse control, poor task performance)

- Reduced dopamine receptors, cravings impaired

Neuroimaging research shows excessive screen time damages the brain.[82]

There are many similar studies available on the side effects of screen time, and more are coming out almost weekly. As our children are plugged in at younger and younger ages, we all need to understand that we are compromising the healthy development of their brains.

Melatonin ("The Sleepy Hormone")

Many preschoolers are taught the "Green Light, Red Light" nursery rhyme so they understand what to do at a stoplight. Red is stop, yellow is wait, green is go. It is time to teach them what a blue light can do to their sleep cycle. Blue light—it's not for night!

As if early onset dementia and anxiety issues were not enough, we have another huge, troubling side effect of too much screen time: chronic sleep deprivation. This phenomenon is relatively new to modern-day society and is primarily caused by the blue light emitted from our screens, especially when used in the evening.

> The blue light emitted from your phone screen can actually keep you awake longer than drinking a double espresso before bed!

How many of us can correctly answer the question "what color is white light?" Drum roll . . . . . . and the answer is: *ALL OF THEM.*[83] The natural daylight emitted from the sun is actually made up of all the colors of the visual spectrum, with the color blue having a little more dominance than the other colors. Natural sunlight is a good source of vitamin D and can help our mood and our attention span; it also serves to suppress the hormone melatonin. (Yes, another hormone you can teach your kids.)

In addition to the hormones cortisol and dopamine previously discussed, the body secretes the hormone melatonin, which is commonly referred to as the "sleep-regulating hormone." Melatonin is produced by the pineal gland, makes you feel tired and sleepy, and serves to regulate your circadian rhythm. But what does melatonin have to do with screens? "Most of today's devices are illuminated by LEDs, which have a much higher percentage of blue light waves than any other light source, natural or artificial. Surprisingly, while your screen may look white, the white LED light is actually a blue light which is combined with a chemical to make it look white."[84]

While blue light is acceptable in the daytime, it can wreak havoc when we are exposed to it at night. When you are on your screens, melatonin production comes to a screeching halt. Blue light hits the eyes and sends a message to the pineal gland to stop producing melatonin.[85] Suppression of this vital hormone can affect both the quantity and quality of sleep. "The blue light emitted from your phone screen can actually keep you awake longer than drinking a double espresso before bed!"[86] While many parents allow their children to surf their social media accounts before bed, we wouldn't dream of giving them coffee—yet that's exactly what their screens are doing to their natural sleep cycle. It's like living in a constant state of jet lag.

There are numerous studies on the negative side effects of screen use on sleep. In 2012 a study released by the Lighting Research Center found that exposure to the self-luminous, backlit displays of smartphones, computers, and LED devices suppressed melatonin by 22 percent.[87] A study published in *Scientific American* had volunteers spend several evenings reading for a prolonged period of time before an imposed ten o'clock bedtime. Some used printed books, while some used light-emitting e-readers. The results of the study showed those who used e-readers took longer to fall asleep, had less REM sleep, and felt sleepier and less alert for hours after they woke up in the morning—even if they had gotten the same amount of sleep as those who read print books.[88] Sleep experts say that teens should get about nine hours of sleep a night. A teen who is getting fewer than seven hours a night is significantly sleep-deprived—and 57 percent more teens were sleep-deprived in 2015 than in 1991. Sleep deprivation is linked to a myriad of issues, including compromised thinking and reasoning, susceptibility to illness, weight gain, and high blood pressure. It also affects mood: people who don't sleep enough are prone to depression and anxiety.[90]

Without a major revolution, it seems almost impossible to get a good night's sleep with all the temptations available. Kids don't even remember what it's like to get a long, uninterrupted, rejuvenating, healing night of deep sleep. But rest assured, it is possible to keep our screens and still get proper rest. We just need to change a few of the habits we've gotten used to and take advantage of some of the great new products on the market to help cut out the blue light effect. Look for these in the final solutions chapter.

Dangers of Electromagnetic Fields (EMFs)

No, I'm not going to tell you that a cell phone is like microwave radiation; that is not the issue here. Many experts do not view cell phone exposure as an issue because they are only looking at the thermal (i.e. heat) impacts of cell phones and how our bodies absorb the radio-frequency energy. They claim there is no biological effect since the energy coming from the fields is too low to heat our tissues. This logic is flawed because it ignores the non-thermal effects from cell phones, which are dangerous to adults and to children. We can't see it, but we are drowning in the invisible waters that are EMFs.

If your cell phone is turned on, it's emitting potentially harmful EMFs. Period. "Twenty to eighty percent of the radiation from a phone's antenna penetrates up to two inches into the adult brain. Studies have shown that people who sleep with a cell phone by the bed have poor REM sleep, leading to impaired learning and memory. When the cell phone signal is held next to the head, brainwaves are altered a full 70 percent of the time. Many insurance companies are so alarmed by the emerging evidence of cell phone radiation that they now exclude its related health issues from coverage. Most brain surgeons limit their cell phone use, and counsel patients never to hold them to their ears."[91]

As with Silicon Valley tech execs, we're seeing another common theme here—the experts are doing different things than we are. If brain surgeons limit their cell phone use and tell their patients to do the same, shouldn't we?

How our cell phones actually work is one of those mysteries like how a potato can turn on a light bulb (shout out to my son's science fair project). Some things are better left to the scientists—but not this one. When you make a call or text or use data on your cell phone, here's what happens:

Your phone sends radiofrequency (RF) waves from its antenna to nearby cell towers, and receives RF waves in return to its antenna.[92]

If you are holding the phone next to your face, as most people do, then about 70 percent of the energy from the antenna is absorbed straight into your head.[93]

As you can see from the diagram below, age makes a difference in how much of this energy can be absorbed into the tissue. A younger child's skull is much thinner than an adult's and still developing, and therefore more radiation is able to penetrate the brain. It's not until around age twenty that your brain is fully developed.[94]

As you move your cell phone away from your head, this radiation decreases rapidly. So, clearly, the farther away from your body you can keep your phone, the better.

These visual images should serve as a powerful reminder to parents that it's never a good idea to allow a child to talk on a cell phone held close to the head![95]

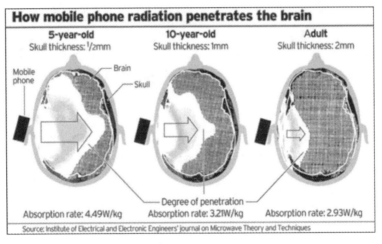

96

To see if my personal cell phone manufacturer had any precautionary warnings about this, I did some digging. Sure enough, my phone itself had a warning that said:

To reduce exposure to RF energy, use a hands-free option, such as the built-in speakerphone, the supplied headphones, or other similar accessories. Cases with metal parts may change the RF performance of the device, including its compliance with RF exposure guidelines, in a manner that has not been tested or certified.

Check your own phone—mine is an iPhone 7.0 and I found the warning with the following steps:

Settings > General > About > Legal > RF Exposure

Or go to www.apple.com/legal/rfexposure.

So how big a problem is this? Not only are we on our cell phones all day long, but many people actually sleep with them in their beds! In fact, it's estimated that 60 percent of adults keep their phone next to them when they sleep. In another survey, half the respondents claimed they check their emails during the night![97] You know who you are (#workingfrombed).

In addition, Dr. Joseph Mercola weighs in on the topic of EMFs. He has authored numerous books on the *New York Times* bestseller list and is the founder of the #1 natural health site Mercola.com. He says that EMF exposure may also increase a man's risk for infertility if he wears his cell phone near his groin and/or uses a laptop on his lap, and a woman's risk for breast cancer is higher if she tucks her phone into her bra. Studies have linked low-level electromagnetic radiation (EMR) exposure from cell phones to an 8 percent reduction in sperm motility and a 9 percent reduction in sperm viability.[98] I'm not going to go into a lot of detail here, since Dr. Mercola is the expert and is coming out with a new book on the dangers of cell phone use and EMFs. Stay tuned.

To analyze another potential danger, it's time for us to take a trip down memory lane, back to high school biology class. The good ol' days . . .

Mitochondria are those little cell powerhouses that produce energy after they combine the food we eat with oxygen we breathe. They also determine the speed at which your body ages. The average adult has 10 million billion—about one billion would fit on the head of a pin.[99] When this whole energy process goes awry, free radicals form and can wreak havoc on our health. Free radicals are linked to over sixty diseases, including Alzheimer's and cancer. Most of all, they accelerate the aging process.

Your body uses electrical fields to communicate between your cells. The electromagnetic fields emitted by the phones are far more damaging to your body because they interfere with your body's own cellular communication.[100] There's a lot more detail here on intracellular calcium on Dr. Mercola's website if you would like more information.

Class B Carcinogen

Many of you may be familiar with Dave Asprey, the founder of Bulletproof Coffee and writer of the book of the same name. Bulletproof Coffee, a mix of coffee and coconut oil or butter, is my favorite way to start the day. Our brains need healthy fats! Dave Asprey is famous for being a biohacker—a person who seeks to change their environment from the inside out so they have full control of their personal biology. Dr. Mercola interviewed Asprey, who told of how he used to keep his cell phone in a pants pocket on his right leg. Asprey now has 10 percent less bone density in his right femur, which he believes is related to carrying his phone there. Needless to say, he no longer carries his phone on his body. I told this to my husband, another Bulletproof Coffee fan—his first response was, "Guess I need to start switching pockets." #uphillbattle

Possibly the biggest blow to the tech industry came when the International Agency for Research on Cancer (IARC), an arm of the World Health Organization (WHO), declared cell phones a Class B Carcinogen, meaning a "possible cancer-causing agent." What else is in class B? Diesel engine exhaust, some pesticides, and some heavy metals. The expert panel ruled that there was some evidence that regular cell phone use increased the risk of two types of tumors—brain tumors (gliomas) and acoustic tumors (neuromas). "Research has shown that those who begin using cell phones heavily before age twenty have four to five times more [risk of] brain cancer by their late twenties, compared to those whose exposure is minimal."[101] Another case to limit cell phone use in children.

Digital Eye Strain (a.k.a. Computer Vision Syndrome)

When we stare at computer screens and other devices all day long, we are overworking the ciliary muscle, which is in the back of the eye. Our eyes feel most comfortable looking around twenty feet away. When we look at things close up, like a cell phone screen, this muscle has to constantly adjust back and forth. "The American Optometric Association estimates that 50 to 90 percent of computer users suffer symptoms of CVS."[102] In addition, 70 percent of millennials report symptoms of digital eye strain.[103] Prolonged screen exposure can lead to dry eyes, headaches, blurred vision, eye fatigue, and retinal damage similar to age-related macular degeneration.

Remember when we talked about South Korea boasting one of the largest populations with smartphones? Just recently, "the ministry of education reports that more than 70 percent of tenth graders have eyesight problems, something doctors attribute to xerophthalmia, or dry eyes, which results from prolonged staring into screens without blinking."[104] The good news is, there are a few easy fixes to protect your eyes, which we will discuss in the chapter on solutions.

Physical Changes: "Text Neck" or "Hump Back"

Your phone doesn't just change your brain; it can also damage your body, especially when you spend hours hunched over your device. We've all seen images of the gambler slumped over the slot machine, eyes glazed, zoned out, doing pull after pull waiting for that elusive jackpot. Are our teens much different, hunched over their phones swipe after swipe?

> We've all seen images of the gambler slumped over the slot machine, eyes glazed, zoned out, doing pull after pull waiting for that elusive jackpot. Are our teens much different, hunched over their phones swipe after swipe?

The average head weights ten to twelve pounds. The weight more than doubles when your head is tilted forward only 15 degrees. Worse yet, most people tilt 60 degrees when on their phones, which equates to a sixty-pound force on your neck! This is often called "text neck" or "turtle neck."[105]

"This is especially concerning because young, growing children could possibly cause permanent damage to their cervical spines that could lead to lifelong neck pain."[106] Common symptoms include upper-back pain, upper-back muscle spasms, shoulder pain, and arm and hand pain caused by a pinched cervical nerve.

We will be giving solutions to help alleviate these symptoms in our last chapter—in a nutshell, #LookUp.

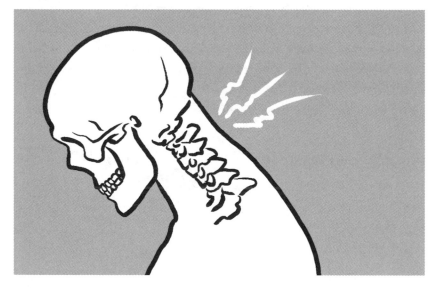

Wrap Up

I know this chapter was very technical and hard to get through, and for that I offer my sincere apology. But when you start to implement the solutions I will outline, you need to be armed with the data and information to let our kids know what the physiological and psychological effects of too much screen time are on their bodies. We are married to our technology, and it's time to cut this ball and chain, one unhealthy habit at a time.

Chapter III

Multitasking: It's a Myth

The current generation has their fair share of labels—Generation Me, the Selfie Generation, Generation Z—but perhaps the one most fitting to describe today's youth is the Multitasking Generation. At present, kids are proud to be scrolling, swiping, texting, and snapping while eating, talking, studying, and streaming. A whopping 97 percent of Generation Z has a smartphone[1], and multitasking is their mode of operation. They type as they talk and read as they chat. These digital natives feel a sense of superiority over the older generation for this unique talent and wear the label like a badge of courage.

Although the younger generation think they are rock stars at successfully multitasking, it turns out that multitasking is an illusion. It's distraction masquerading as productivity. When we multitask, both tasks suffer. For example, I'm notorious for cooking and talking on the phone at the same time. Inevitably, I lose focus and cannot remember if I put that teaspoon of salt in my dish, or have to ask my aunt to repeat what she just said since the listening part of my brain was on pause while my visual processing system was reading the recipe. Kids today repeat this scenario all day long, the ultimate multitasking on steroids.

In its simplest form, *Merriam-Webster* defines multitasking as "the performance of multiple tasks at one time."[2] The specific form of multitasking that gets the most media attention is the potentially deadly scenario of texting and driving. However, according to the American Psychological Association, there are actually three types of multitasking:

- "Performing two tasks simultaneously. This includes talking on the phone while driving or answering email during a webinar."[3]

- "Switching from one task to another without completing the first task. We've all been right in the middle of focused work when an urgent task demands our attention; this is one of the most frustrating kinds of multitasking, and often the hardest to avoid."[4]

- "Performing two or more tasks in rapid succession. It almost doesn't seem like multitasking at all, but our minds need time to change gears in order to work efficiently."[5]

Of course a computer can perform multiple processes at the same time or switch back and forth effortlessly, but the human brain cannot. This is one of those rare research facts that everyone in the scientific community agrees on. Multitasking is a myth that people continue to perpetuate (kind of like the myth that morning sickness only happens in the morning—lots of experience on this one). Perpetuating the multitasking myth is self-serving, as it allows people to continue their frantic yapping and driving, convinced that they are being productive. There is ample research to show that multitasking does not exist. Here is a "CliffsNotes" synopsis, with sources provided if you'd like to dig deeper:

"While the human body can multitask in the sense that we do things like breathe and walk at the same time, a vast difference exists between functions that we can do automatically—breathing, blinking, and some mindless tasks like washing dishes—and those functions that require attention and focus. In short, our brains are actually incapable of multitasking because we can only pay meaningful mental attention to one thing at a time."[6]

MIT neuroscientist Earl Miller states, "People can't multitask very well, and when people say they can, they're deluding themselves, the brain is very good at deluding itself."[7]

Stanford professor Clifford Nass says, "We, so far, have not found people who are successful at multitasking. There's some evidence that there's a very, very, very, very small group of people who can do two tasks at one time, but there's actually no evidence anyone can do three."[8]

It's estimated that only 2 percent of the population is actually proficient at multitasking, and ironically, these people are the least likely to actually multitask. The problem is that we all think we're part of that 2 percent, and use our perceived ability as justification to juggle too many tasks. "Perceptions of the ability to multitask were found to be badly inflated; in fact, the majority of participants judged themselves to be above average in the ability to multitask. These estimations had little grounding in reality as perceived multitasking ability was not significantly correlated with actual multitasking ability."[9]

German neurologist Dr. Spitzer says that in a strict sense, humans cannot multitask. You can't read two books at once, talk to two different people at once, or run two different kinds of content at the same time, yet that's just what computers are demanding from you. That's the essence of what our screens are asking us to do.[10]

So what is really happening when we pretend we are masters at juggling five tasks at once? We are really just switchtasking. We switch our attention from task to task extremely quickly, starting and stopping over and over again. There's a Buddhist term for this switchtasking—it's called "Monkey Mind." It refers to a state of being "unsettled, restless, inconstant, or confused [. . .] Just as a monkey jumps from tree to tree, our minds switch from thought to thought, leaving us distracted and disorganized."[11]

Just as there's no such thing as a free lunch, switchtasking comes at a great price. Our brain is working in overdrive trying to shift focus between multiple tasks, and the constant back-and-forth affects our performance at home, school, and work. In choosing to divide our attention, the switching costs include, but are not limited to, lessened cognitive ability, loss in productivity, and mental and behavioral changes.

Lessened Cognitive Ability

Your phone has the same privileged status as your name.[12]

The concept I am about to describe is probably one of the most important takeaways from this book. It's backed by numerous scientific studies, most notably research performed by psychologist Adrian Ward at the University of Texas–Austin.

In a nutshell, Ward and his team conclude, "[We] have limited attentional resources, and we use some of them to point the rest of those resources in the right direction. Usually different things are important in different contexts, but some things—like your name—have a really privileged status."[13] (Say the name "Judy" in a crowd and I automatically turn my head.) "This idea with smartphones is that it's similarly relevant all of the time, and it also gets this privileged attentional space. [. . .] In other words, if you grow dependent on your smartphone, it becomes a magical device that silently shouts your name at your brain at all times."[14]

"In the study, Ward and his colleagues examined the performance of more than five hundred undergraduates on two different common psychological

Your phone has the same privileged status as your name.

tests of memory and attention. In the first experiment, some participants were told to set their phones to silent without vibration and either leave them in their bag or put them on their desk. Other participants were asked to leave all their possessions, including their cell phone, outside the testing room. In the second experiment, students were asked to leave their phones on their desk, in their bag, or out in the hall, just as in the first experiment. But some students were also asked to power their phone off, regardless of location. In both experiments, students who left their phones outside the room seemed to do best on the test. They also found the trials easier."[15]

> Multitasking lowers your actual IQ.

Why is this? "Attractive objects draw attention, and it takes mental energy to keep your attention focused when a desirable distractor is nearby. Put a chocolate cake on the table next to a dieter . . . and we would expect them to have a bit more trouble on whatever they're supposed to be doing."[16]

Another study showed that having a phone just sitting on your desk at school is hard not only on the owner of the phone but on other students as well because their brains are just waiting for something to happen. "It's a distraction for all."[17] Sounds like the modern-day form of secondhand smoke!

With all this information about reduced brainpower caused by our cell phones, it makes a person wonder if we as a society are making phones smarter and people dumber. Unfortunately, the research confirms it: multitasking lowers your actual IQ. This is one of the most astonishing and depressing facts I've read during my research. All the overstimulation resulting from multitasking is causing mental fatigue, and it's especially damaging on growing and developing teen brains.

"A study at the University of London found that participants who multitasked during cognitive tasks experienced IQ score declines that were similar to what they'd expect if they had smoked marijuana or stayed up all night! IQ drops of fifteen points for multitasking men lowered their scores to the average range of an eight-year-old child."[18] Instead of "Are you smarter than a fifth grader?" we're moving to "Are you smarter than an eight-year-old?" Another study shows that workers distracted by emails and phone calls suffer a fall in their IQ that is twice what is found in marijuana smokers. I guess we'd better hope our kids aren't in college on their phones and multitasking while smoking weed!

Multitasking is a public health hazard, and it has cost us thousands of lives. Another very visible illustration of decreased cognitive ability when doing multiple tasks at once is the sad statistics surrounding smartphone usage while driving. Cell phone use can pose a serious safety risk for those who choose to text, talk on the phone, or even use a navigation system while driving.

I saw an alarming billboard in a cornfield on one of our recent road trips. It displayed five short words:

BETTER LEFT UNREAD THAN **DEAD**

> Most of us wouldn't dare drink and drive, yet texting while driving is commonplace and is "6X more likely to cause an accident than driving drunk."

It caught my eye (thankfully, I was the passenger); the blood-red color of the word "DEAD" was especially unsettling. When I got home, I looked into the message and found out it was part of the #StopTextsStopWrecks campaign sponsored by the National Highway Traffic Safety Administration (NHTSA).[19] Sadly, text message memorials have become all too common as a driver's last words, immortalized on the frozen screen of their cell phone. As a parent of four teen drivers, I can tell you this is the driving lesson I prayed would sink in the most for my kids. I never ever worried they would drink and drive, but I did worry about texting and driving. I still pray every day they heed my advice and never touch their phones when driving.

The number of distracted driving deaths has skyrocketed over the years, making the impact of our cell phones on the number of auto wrecks statistically undeniable.

- Nearly 390,000 injuries occur each year from accidents caused by texting while driving.[20]

- 1 out of every 4 car accidents in the United States is caused by texting and driving.[21]

- According to a AAA poll, 94 percent of teen drivers acknowledge the dangers of texting and driving, but 35 percent admit to doing it anyway.[22]

- 21 percent of teen drivers involved in fatal accidents were distracted by their cell phones.[23]

- Teen drivers are four times more likely than adults to get into car crashes or near crashes when talking or texting on a cell phone.[24]

Keep in mind, all these statistics are despite forty-one states having laws against driving and cell phone use, some stricter than others. Most of us wouldn't dare drink and drive, yet texting while driving is commonplace and is "6X more likely to cause an accident than driving drunk."[25] There are three types of distracted driving: visual (taking your eyes off the road), manual (taking your hands off the wheel), and cognitive (taking your mind off driving).[26] Texting while driving is so dangerous because it involves all three types of distraction.

Quickly reading or responding to a text message might only take five seconds, but "if you are traveling down a highway at fifty-five miles per hour, that's enough time to travel the full length of a football field."[27] Imagine what you could miss. I think this is an example of the "not me" phenomenon. We all think that we are masters at driving and using our cell phones, that the statistics don't apply to us. But few of us are part of the elite 2 percent who can multitask. And even if you are, it's arrogant, risky, and illegal—so just don't do it! A car can injure or kill you or someone else, and talking or texting on the phone is never worth that.

I will provide the most recent recommended solutions to this problem in my last chapter. We must teach our kids that any cell phone use when operating a motor vehicle is worse than drunk driving. They just cannot do it, and neither should we.

Loss in Productivity

While I recognize it may be impossible to completely eliminate this multitasking monster, with education on how much brain power we are sacrificing and productive work time we are losing, maybe society will make the changes necessary to reduce the negative effects. When we are juggling multiple tasks, we become less effective at school, home, or work. Every time we switch tasks, we lose momentum, a phenomenon I think most of us can't deny.

"Research conducted at Stanford University found that multitasking is less productive than doing a single thing at a time. The researchers found that people who are regularly bombarded with several streams of electronic information cannot pay attention, recall information, or switch from one job to another as well as those who complete one task at a time. [. . .] The frequent multitaskers performed worse because they had more trouble organizing their thoughts and filtering out irrelevant information, and they were slower at switching from one task to another."[28]

So how much time do we lose when we are trying to multitask and end up distracted? The *Harvard Business Review* published a compelling article called "You Can't Multitask, So Stop Trying." The author concluded that, based on over a half-century of cognitive science and more recent studies on multitasking, it takes an average of fifteen minutes to reorient to a primary task after a distraction such as an email. Long-term memory suffers, creativity is reduced, and efficiency can drop by as much as 40 percent.[29]

Other research suggests that the range of disruption is anywhere from four to twenty-five minutes, depending on the distraction and the participant. Even if it's just on the low end, checking your phone five times in an hour means twenty minutes of reduced productivity with your brain trying to reorient to the task at hand. It's no wonder high school kids who study with their phones near them are up until midnight trying to get everything done.

Mental and Behavioral Changes

Dividing our attention affects not only our productivity and safety, but also how we see and treat those around us. "Simply having a cell phone nearby—without even checking it—can reduce empathy."[30]

"Researchers at the University of Sussex in the UK compared the amount of time people spend on multiple devices (such as texting while watching TV) to MRI scans of their brains. They found that high multitaskers had less brain density in the anterior cingulate cortex, a region responsible for empathy as well as cognitive and emotional control."[31] There are some brain chemicals at work, since scientists show that not only is multitasking an impediment to learning, it can also prompt the release of stress hormones such as cortisol and adrenaline.[32] Recall from our medical chapter, cortisol is the fight-or-flight hormone and contributes to our children's anxiety, keeping the so-called "Always On" generation in a state of high alert. It's like their brains have ten tabs open at once—and they are scrambling just to keep up.

Another behavioral change is related to what our eyes are doing when they try to keep up with what's presented on our devices. Since the beginning of time, our brains have been wired to deal with visual stimulation that occurs in nature—not the frantic, rapid-fire visual changes on today's screens that have only emerged in the last decade. Our children appear on the surface to have no trouble keeping up, but internally their brains are working in high gear to process all the content from rapidly changing screens.

Many parents report that when their kids are playing a video game or on their iPad, they are actually in a hyperfocused state, especially if the child has ADHD. Their visual processing system is completely focused on keeping up with the changing images. But what happens when you pull them away from this eye candy on their screen? Pandemonium breaks loose; if they were super-focused before, they are now super-unfocused. They're hyper. They act out. They're in an awful mood.

A crash occurs. Until their brain adjusts to real life and a normal pace, which takes time, your child will be bouncing off the walls in an unconscious attempt to find stimuli moving at the artificially fast pace of his brain.[33]

There's another internal mechanism affected as well—the vestibular system, often called our sixth sense. This is a complicated sensory system in our inner ear that provides balance and spatial orientation. I'm very familiar with this, since I have had vertigo since I was very young and often have bouts of motion sickness. Everyone is different in how much stimulation they can take; some can read and ride in the back seat of a car in heavy traffic while others have to keep their eyes on the road. For most people, rotational acceleration of the vestibular system, like a rapidly scrolling screen, is arousing, while linear acceleration, like being rocked as a baby, is calming. Our brains are often confused because of the discrepancy between what our eyes are seeing and what our body is feeling. This digital motion sickness is magnified by the recent invention of virtual reality goggles. When our kids spend time on screens, we have to help them come out of the super-focused state and reset their visual and vestibular systems. I have a way to ease your child off their screens in the solutions chapter.

Although multitasking is often upheld as a signal of productivity and hard work, the reality is more sinister. Multitasking with our screens makes us dumber, more distracted, and less safe. I also mentioned that multitasking could make us less empathetic—but empathy isn't the only virtue that screen time can detract from. Smartphones don't just affect our minds and our bodies; they can affect the development of our children's virtues and character.

Chapter IV

Where Have All the Virtues Gone?

Now that we have covered how digital technology is affecting our children on a physiological level, let's move on to some early warning signs of changes in the moral character and value system of the plugged-in generation. To me, the largest contributor to a person's character is the virtues they strive to attain as they go about their daily life, big decisions and small. I think of virtues as those habits or attitudes we have that dictate our conduct, largely with a disposition toward good works. Think of what you want people to say during the eulogy at your funeral. It's not the work skills we obtain that people remember us for, but how we lived our life and the relationships we built.

I truly believe that kids today are fundamentally good. I see evidence of this time and time again in my own children and their friends. I am very fortunate to live in a community with a great school system, plenty of neighborhood parks, a strong faith culture, and very little crime. We are

> An alarming recent survey stated that 60 percent of adults believe that young people's failure to learn moral values is a serious national problem.

truly blessed. But even though we live in this little bubble we call "Chanhappening," I'm not so naïve as to think we're immune to negative societal influences like drugs, entitlement, cyberbullying, online pornography, or teen suicide. These do happen in my community and around the world.

I believe the moral compass of this generation is shifting, more south than north, as children's characters are increasingly shaped by their smartphones and social media in particular. An alarming recent survey stated that 60 percent of adults believe that young people's failure to learn moral values is a serious national problem. Another survey put this number at 72 percent.[1] It's hard to tell if there truly is a moral crisis among an entire generation of teens or if the ones with questionable characters are so widely reported online that we feel there is a crisis. Perception is reality?

Regardless, countless notable public figures do not seem to understand the difference between right and wrong, and their daily indiscretions are viewed online by millions. Professional athletes and Hollywood starlets and actors often seem like they are above the common laws of society. #MeToo.

Notice the survey said "failure to learn moral values." To me, this is the pivotal shift that has occurred; our children's primary influences are shifting from us, their parents, to their smartphones. The influence of real people is diminishing, and their belief system is significantly influenced by what is on their screen.

How did this change in the moral compass happen, and at such lightning speed? First and foremost, a large portion of the blame has to lie squarely on the shoulders of my fellow parents and me—we are the ones who have created this generation. I'm not trying to shame here, but at some point, we have to take ownership of where we are in order to make changes. We run their lunch to school when they forget it, we fill out their college applications, we wrap them in bubble wrap so they don't get hurt. Yet the biggest threat to their health and happiness, this supercomputer disguised as a toy, we allow them to use 24-7, with many households having few boundaries or rules whatsoever.

We are the ones who buy the phones and pay the monthly contract fees. We are the ones who have every intention of installing parental controls but never get around to it. We are the ones letting our children spend so much time on their phones, using their devices as virtual babysitters. And we are the ones who are too busy looking down to look up. "Distracted parents cultivate distracted children."[2]

A lot of today's generational shift can be attributed to changes in family structure and finances. Many households have both parents working, and neither one feels as though they have enough time to spend raising their children. This is especially true for single working parents, who are often forced to allow kids an extraordinary amount of free time at home given the high costs of daycare. I know how this feels, as I was a single mother for ten years and the majority of my paycheck went to childcare expenses. My two oldest kids were raised by me, my dad, and my "village" of helpers (you know who you are—thank you!).

However, these latchkey children often turn to their devices, video games in particular, when left alone. Many of these youths are playing very violent games that are desensitizing them and slowly eroding their sense of empathy. "The more kids see and experience violence (whether at school, home, on TV, computer, video games, or as a victim), the more they think it's 'normal, common, and acceptable.' And the more it lowers kids' inhibitions against aggression toward others."[3]

The expectations parents have for children today have also dramatically changed from a generation or two ago. More than ever before, we are a society of Tiger Moms and helicopter parents raising a generation of self-centered, entitled, and competitive youth. We have built an entire generation for whom high achievement in academics and sports is valued more than being kind. Most children spend significantly more time being shuffled around for travel sports than they do helping others in the community.

Take heart—all is not doom and gloom. There is hope to change the trajectory we are on. We can't turn back to a time before screens were in every home and office, but we can put screen usage in its place within the larger context of our lives and our children's lives. The time for changes in our behavior is now, by adopting one habit at a time until cell phones take the backseat to more important personal relationships and ventures in our lives. We have to get our bolt cutters out and free our children from this electronic leash weighing them down. We have taught our kids so many important lessons—don't talk to strangers, don't run with scissors, eat your veggies, look both ways before you cross the street—but we also need to teach them the lost virtues with an intentional and concerted effort. The way to do this is addressed in my solutions chapter, but first, let's drill down to some important virtues and get a sense of how today's kids are measuring up.

Temperance

By definition, the virtue of temperance is "moderation or self-restraint, self-control."[4] To act moderately is to act within reasonable limits, not to give in to excess.

Pope Gregory is one of the famous Catholic Church leaders I like to study, since my youngest son is named Gregory. I will never forget when he was seven years old and donned his robe and mitre to dress as Pope Gregory at school for All Saints Day. (A mitre is a tall, folded hat with a top that looks like a fish's mouth.) Pope Gregory has some inspired commentary that applies not just to Catholics but to all mankind. He defined temperance as "moderation of needed things and abstinence from things which are not needed."[5] Of course, he was largely referring to a self-indulgent existence in relation to our appetite for sex and food. Today's application goes far beyond these two temptations, and the desire to touch the computer makes it almost impossible to moderate or rein in.

Aren't the lines between needs and wants getting fairly blurred at this point—or even flipped upside down? Historically, food, shelter, and transportation have been the basic human needs. But now, many people would pay their cell phone bill before even their mortgage or car payment. There are developing countries that have more cell phones than working toilets. Think of the days during the Great Depression, World Wars I and II, and even the recent recession in 2007. People were hunkering down and mainly concerned with keeping a roof over their heads and putting food on their tables, not which Netflix shows they could binge watch for hours on end or how they could come up with $500 for the newest cell phone. As a child, I vividly remember wearing the Wonder Bread empty plastic bag inside my boots to act as a boot liner in winter. Maybe that's a Wisconsin thing, but we all were doing it, so it didn't seem strange at the time. Could you imagine how kids today would revolt if we told them to wear used bread-loaf bags in their boots to keep their socks dry, or to help squeeze into last season's boots that are too small? Dry feet in Wisconsin winters seem like a necessity.

I would argue that most children right now think having a smartphone with unlimited data is also a necessity, not the luxury it was even just a few years ago. For some, I would go as far to say their phone is actually like a body part; they cannot be anywhere without it, including their bathroom and their bed. As a society, we are addicted and cannot live without our devices—we don't just want them, we *need* them. Teens can go weeks without being able to find their winter coat in the frozen tundra of Minnesota, but can't go five minutes without knowing where their phone is.

Let me illustrate needs vs. wants with one of my favorite passions: food. Many ten- to twelve-year-old boys live on the "beige" diet, where everything on their plate is beige or brown: chicken nuggets, hamburgers, pizza, french fries, Coca Cola, potato chips, cookies, or macaroni and cheese. Ugh, my stomach is hurting just thinking of all that junk. This is clearly the opposite of the colors of the rainbow present with fresh fruits and vegetables. The beige diet would have been the preferred diet for my boys if I'd let them—but, as parents, do we allow our children to eat junk food and processed food 24-7? No, we tell them to eat their veggies, an apple, scrambled eggs, a salad, a handful of nuts, or a smoothie. (Can you tell I believe in "farmacy" to stay healthy, not "pharmacy"? "Let food be thy medicine!") Don't get me wrong, I make a mean chocolate-chip cookie—but my kids eat that *only* after eating a healthy dinner. Children and their screens are the same. We need to start thinking of what's really good for their growing brains and their bodies in the long run, not just what they may want at the present moment.

Temperance was one of Ben Franklin's thirteen virtues—in fact, it is this virtue that gave him the self-discipline to live the other twelve. When Ben Franklin spoke of the virtue of temperance he was mainly referring to avoiding overindulgences in food and drink: "Eat not to dullness; drink not to elevation."[6] In other words, we need to control our appetite. The alternative is giving in to gluttony.

Appetite in itself isn't a bad thing—it's really a built-in survival mechanism so that we do eat and thrive. But even something good can turn into something damaging, which is what has happened with the Standard American Diet, our overindulgence on sugar, and the resultant rise in diabesity. To me, temperance in today's generation and the modern-day form of gluttony go far beyond just food; they can also be applied to excessive indulgences in relation to our attention.

Silicon Valley engineers are paid a lot of money to make cell phones addictive so you give them your constant attention; a high level of engagement is their business model. That translates to more money for the cell phone manufacturers, advertisers, web designers, and data companies. It makes sense when you consider that "98 percent of Facebook's revenue comes from advertising, totaling $39.9 billion last year alone."[7] The gluttonous monsters that are sucking up all of our time and attention drastically change our behaviors and expectations courtesy of three main drivers: too much information, too many different choices and targeted data feeds, and instant gratification.

We are pulled in countless directions every few minutes, sometimes even every few seconds. Answer this text, read this email, like this photo, watch this cute little cat video. The volume of digital information thrown at us all day is overwhelming. How many times have we had to scroll through screen after screen just looking for the one thing we wanted to read? It's maddening and such a waste of time. With all the information thrown at us, many are becoming passive consumers of knowledge, opting to read articles because they conveniently popped up on the screen with little or no intent or purpose.

My childhood idol was Jackie Kennedy. I read every book I could get my hands on about her. Jackie was as famous for her intellect and knowledge of history and the arts as she was for her unique beauty. When her husband was a rising senator, she went back to college to take courses in foreign service and international relations so she could understand more of her husband John F. Kennedy's world. I'm not saying I expect kids to have the standards of an accomplished woman with thorough knowledge of modern languages, the arts, history, and literature, but I also think we can't just be lulled into a passive consumption of the knowledge that the technology giants target for us on our phones. We need to be more deliberate in and conscious of our media selection.

Beside the sheer volume of digital information coming at us, with an unlimited data plan also comes an enormous number of choices. One swipe and your kid's phone can do as much computing as an entire room of computers for the Apollo 13 journey![8] Did you know there are currently a billion different websites?[9] Not to mention thousands and thousands of music and movie choices.

Smartphones give our kids so many choices to begin with, and their own surfing activity completely customizes their screens to their preferences courtesy of data mining by Facebook, Google, Yahoo, and the other big monopolies. The advertisers have developed scarily accurate algorithms to show us what we want, even before we know we want it. For example, Google has a personalized advertisement profile on each user. Based on your individual data—location, gender, age, work, interests, relationship status, income, health concerns, future plans, and so on—Google creates personalized advertisements that might interest you. Have you ever done a search for a particular product or service and suddenly found yourself flooded with ads for that precise thing? That's your data profile at work. If you want this to end, you can choose to opt out of the targeted advertisement or customize what ads you see at "Google's ads settings."[10]

By allowing kids unlimited access to their screens, we promote entitlement and the illusion that the world really does revolve around them. Having almost thirty years of parenting experience, I can tell there's a phase where all teens around age fifteen think the world *does* revolve around them, and that's a natural part of the maturation process. Have faith, they do outgrow this stage! But it's not normal to have seven-year-olds, ten-year-olds, or twenty-five-year-olds acting like this.

Perhaps most damaging of all is that we live in a continual state of instant gratification. With each new day, faster methods of delivering information appear, yet we still grow impatient to have everything right at our fingertips. Siri and Alexa answer fast, Uber picks you up fast, Amazon packages come fast, and Jimmy John's delivers freaky fast. You don't even have to wait for snail mail anymore—the US Postal Service just rolled out "informed delivery" so you can digitally preview what's coming in your mailbox the next day.[11]

Because kids are so used to getting what they want on their phones when they want it, they become impatient and needy when they don't. Our kids' mode of operation is *want, need, now!* And as parents, many promote this instant gratification by immediately responding to our kids' every whim: "I'm hungry"—bam, fast food. "I'm bored"—bam, play a game on my phone . . .

A side effect of this culture of instant gratification and self-indulgence is that many of us have lost the practice of patience. Remember all the little breaks during the day when we used to patiently wait at the stop sign, in line at the grocery store or the post office? And during these down times, we could talk to our neighbors, meet new people in line, or just be silent with our own thoughts. This time is now being replaced with little fillers of checking our email, updating Facebook, and fidgeting. And when we actually have twenty-two minutes of free time, what do we do? We fill them—freaky fast! One of the biggest self-indulgent, instantly gratifying entertainment platforms available right now is streaming video.

I can't call to mind another time when an entire generation of people spent so much time on an activity that was mostly unproductive and merely for entertainment, with little monetary or educational value—binge watching. How many hours do people spend watching their latest guilty pleasure on Netflix or scrolling through countless YouTube videos? Don't get me wrong, I've been known to watch a few episodes of *Poldark* at 2:00 a.m., but not since I've been doing all the screen research on sleep and blue light.

When I was a freshman in college, there was a soap opera the whole country seemed to be watching: *General Hospital*. The buildup to the lead characters' wedding lasted well over a year; we waited months and months for Luke and Laura's wedding. In fact, to this day, their wedding on November 17, 1981, remains the highest-rated soap opera episode in American daytime television history, with thirty million viewers.[12] We skipped class, rearranged our schedules, had viewing parties—there was no Tivo back then. This was the Super Bowl of daytime television, decades before Bachelor Nation was a thing. We talked about it for months before and months after. It was a lesson I learned very early in life: 80 percent of the joy in most things is the anticipation—the actual event is about 20 percent of the fun.

Flash forward thirty-five years, and look at our kids' current viewing experience. It's one thing to say that Netflix, Hulu, and Amazon Prime have replaced our generation's traditional TV viewing on ABC, NBC, and CBS. While this is true for many, the most important change of all was a pivotal shift that occurred five years ago with Netflix. "In August 2012, Netflix introduced a subtle new feature called 'Post-Play.' As one episode ended, the Netflix player automatically loaded the next one, which began playing 5 seconds later."[13] When the credits start to roll, viewers can immediately jump to the next episode. Now you have to decide NOT to watch the next episode. "Most people who binge complete the first season of the shows they're watching in four to six days. A season once stretched on for months at a time—now it's consumed in under a week."[14] The same holds true for movies. Rather than having users go to the main menu and search for their next movie, the post-play experience will bring up recommendations to keep viewers engaged.

What's concerning to me is that with video streaming and binge watching, buildup and anticipation are gone. You can watch the end of an episode with a huge cliffhanger, and bam!—five seconds later, you're on to the next episode. Although this is a subtle change, it truly changes our kids' ability to be patient in anticipation of an event. While that may be fine for a fifty-year-old who has developed lifelong skills of patience and waiting, it's far more damaging for young kids building their personalities. These expectations learned while streaming tend to creep into other facets of our kids' lives. And this does not even address the sheer amount of time wasted doing something that is meant for purely entertainment purposes. Netflix recently announced that users watched one billion hours of content per week in 2017![15]

Temperance is a key virtue that we must pass on to our children. The ability to patiently wait will help our kids conquer their dependence on and addiction to their devices. Learning to delay gratification is a skill they will need if they want to truly be happy and successful in life. Then, when all the stresses of life come—and they will come—our children will be able to handle them much better, because they won't be used to getting what they want when they want it. When I think of all the challenges my family and my friends have endured—long pregnancies and bedrest, illness and death of parents, caring for sick or disabled children, searching for employment, and learning the ropes at new jobs—I don't know how we would have survived without patience. Not to mention amazing experiences that require patience like growing a garden, playing chess, learning a musical instrument, teaching a child to tie his shoes, and potty training.

I will give you suggestions to foster the virtue of temperance and patience in my last chapter. This always-on generation needs to just be offline sometimes. Next, let's move on to one of the most important predictors of our children's success and happiness: empathy.[16]

Empathy

Empathy is "the ability to identify with or understand the perspective, experiences, or motivations of another individual and to comprehend and share another individual's emotional state."[17] In other words, empathizing is putting yourself in another's shoes and understanding what they are feeling.

Are we naturally born to care, or is this something taught to us during our upbringing? Ah, the age-old question: nature vs. nurture. Martin Hoffman, renowned New York University psychologist, believes that the innate predisposition to cry with another "seems to be the

> Violent video games were originally invented for soldiers to desensitize them to what they might see on the battlefield; they served a legitimate purpose.

earliest precursor to empathy."[18] That's why, if you walk into any newborn nursery and one baby is crying, they're all crying.[19] It's called the Wailing Room Phenomenon, and it proves that we are born to care.

Then why does it seem like some kids today can be so unkind? I'm sorry to say, but as a society, *we* kill empathy. Period. This is a learned phenomenon—learned either at home, at school, on the bus, at the playground, or on a screen. Think of what our kids are exposed to on a daily basis. "Our media is called 'the most violent in the world' for good reason. By the end of elementary school, the average child will witness eight thousand murders, and, by age eighteen, two hundred thousand other vivid acts of violence, on all screens."[20]

Boys play an average of 11.3 hours of video games per week, and 40 percent of nine-year-old boys have played *Grand Theft Auto*, a video game series brimming with violence, nudity, foul language, and drug abuse.[21] In the game, the players pose as criminals learning to kill fellow gangsters, police, and even innocent civilians. "In-depth studies from Canada's Brock University found that overexposure to violent images also slows moral growth and weakens a child's ability to feel for others."[22] "Average young people, especially boys, will have played about 10,000 hours of video games by age twenty-one."[23] Our youth are becoming experts in a skill set that has limited use outside itself, except for those who go into the gaming industry or computer simulation. To put this in perspective, "10,000 hours are more than it takes to get a bachelor's degree."[24]

> "Those of us who are older were raised *with* technology, but many of today's young people are being raised *by* technology."

Violent video games were originally invented for soldiers to desensitize them to what they might see on the battlefield; they served a legitimate purpose.[25] Fast forward to 2019, and today we have the ordinary boy next door playing games that were intended for our nation's military—games invented to desensitize them! Brain scans found that just one week after playing violent video games, even kids who were not frequent video game players showed decreased activity in the parts of their brains that regulate emotions, attention, and concentration. These games increase aggressive thoughts and decrease empathy.

Remember when I talked about attending the viewing for *Screenagers*? I was with a group of parents and educators who all watched the movie together. There was a very disturbing scene in the movie when a teen was playing a video game depicting an assault on a woman, which looked eerily realistic. All the parents gasped at the horror of what we were witnessing. At the end of the movie, the school principal came forward and spoke to the group of parents. Sadly, he pointed out that while all of us parents gasped at the violence, when the student body watched the same scene earlier in the day, they laughed. Of course, all our mouths dropped open, and everyone secretly prayed *their* teenager didn't laugh. I imagine there were a lot of conversations at home with kiddos that night.

I read a great quote recently: "Those of us who are older were raised *with* technology, but many of today's young people are being raised *by* technology."[26] Do we really want our kids to learn the virtues of empathy and humility from their screen? Think of all the cyberbullying kids are subjected to on a daily basis. Teens have this keyboard courage to say cruel and unkind things they would never say in person. Sadie Riggs was a teen who hung herself over being bullied at school. In lieu of flowers, the family asked people to just be kind to one another.[27]

A 2014 study showed that cyberbullying incidents had tripled in a single year. A new study shows that teens today are 40 percent less empathetic than teens thirty years ago.[28] Nearly 43 percent of children have been bullied online, but only one in ten will inform a parent or trusted adult of their abuse. One in four middle school students contemplate suicide as a solution to peer cruelty. Legislators are so concerned that all fifty states have passed antibullying policies.[29]

A controversial Netflix show called *13 Reasons Why* attempts to explain how a high school girl came to the conclusion that she should take her own life. The show contained a graphic depiction of her suicide and singles out the classmates that she blames for driving her to this ultimate end. Psychiatrists and mental health professionals have campaigned against the series, saying its sensationalized portrayal of her suicide could encourage young people to take their own lives. Schools across the country have sent letters home to parents encouraging them not to allow their children to watch the series. Dr. Helen Rayner, spokeswoman for the Royal College of Psychiatrists, says the "dramatic and detailed portrayal of suicide needlessly put[s] vulnerable young people at risk of copycat behavior as they see how to carry out harmful or potential fatal acts."[30] I watched this series to preview it in case my fifteen-year-old requested to see it. Yes, the suicide was graphic and disturbing. But equally harmful was the portrayal of rampant sex, drug abuse, rape, gun violence, vulgar language, deceit, and lying to parents. I pray to God this is not what a normal high school social life looks like.

Nor does the bullying stop at a screen. School shootings are a quick reminder of how bad things can get. "So far in 2018, the number of US students killed in school shootings is greater than the number of US military personnel who have been killed on active duty."[31] As of this writing, there has been more than one school shooting a week all year.[32]

The media coverage of these events makes it seem like they happen right in our own neighborhood. Many of us can remember the effect that having televisions in every household had on our perception of the Vietnam War. All at once, it was like people at home were on the front lines of the battlefield and could see firsthand what these soldiers were going through. That's what the internet, social media in particular, has done for school shootings. Many of those involved are filming, snapping, and posting so we can see the horrific event and hear the shooters, which is making kids and parents fearful. As a sign of our troubled times, a group of graduating eighth graders in Pennsylvania were just given ballistics shields as a "welcome to high school" gift.[33] We need to get back to the days before bulletproof backpacks, when our kids could just go to school and parents could know they were safe. This cannot continue to define the United States' education system.

Pygmalion Effect

How do we raise empathetic kids? There is a simple formula: we tell them they're kind and put them in places to show that, starting as early as possible. As parents, we need to create small, teachable moments that become habits practiced over a lifetime. Each time you tell your kid they are kind, they will see themselves as someone who truly cares; eventually, their behavior will match their self-image. Let's look at an example of this theory in practice.

I'm a huge fan of Broadway shows and musical productions, inspired by my high school swing choir days and my role as Ado Annie in *Oklahoma*. I don't think there is one major musical I haven't seen— *The Sound of Music, Seven Brides for Seven Brothers, The Phantom of the Opera, La La Land, A Star is Born*. One of my all-time favorites is *My Fair Lady*. How many times did I twirl around my childhood home singing "I Could Have Danced All Night" or "The Rain in Spain Falls Mainly on the Plain"? The musical is about a speech professor named Henry Higgins who takes a bet that he can't turn a common gal—Eliza Doolittle, who has strong street slang and a twang to her voice—into a high-society lady by teaching her proper dialect. He succeeds, and Eliza debuts her new dialect at the Ascot horse race. She is indeed seen as a high-society lady, and all the young gentlemen vie for her affections.

Why did this experiment work, and what was Mr. Higgins trying to prove? Due to the Pygmalion effect, people will raise or lower themselves to the level you treat them. Put another way, people live up or down to a leader's expectations. And who is the leader in your house? You, Mom and/or Dad. Most of us expect our kids to try hard in school and get good grades—we also need to tell them we expect them to care for others. While many parents do, some fall short.

For some kids, it's easy to step into another's shoes and know how they feel. For others, there's almost an epiphany, a transformational moment that changes them—they suddenly understand something in a very clear way. In this case, you see what it looks like to be kind.[34] Luckily, it's never too late for this transformational moment to occur. You just need to put the kids in the right spot to exercise their empathy muscle, no matter what age. We need to carve out time each week to help others and let our children see themselves as kind. When you help people, it releases a feel-good hormone called serotonin, which gives you a feeling nicknamed the "helper's high." Let's get the serotonin going instead of that dopamine we learned about in the medical chapter!

The Art of Conversation

Day in and day out, our children are prioritizing time on their phone over time with real people. The skill of having a deep conversation and looking someone in the eye seems to be vanishing right before our eyes. Many kids are much more comfortable looking down than looking up at someone face to face. According to Jeane Twenge, kids "can easily click on the perfect emoji in a texting dialogue, but fumble to come up with the appropriate facial expression when they are with real people."[35] Jennifer Aniston, made famous by the sitcom *Friends*, was recently quoted as saying, "If *Friends* was created today, you would have a coffee shop full of people that were just staring into iPhones. There would be no actual episodes or conversations."[36]

Due to the explosion of cell phone addiction and all the time spent on our screens, we have become totally focused on ourselves and are taking time away from building key relationships with family, friends, and the wider community. Kids today prefer texting or posting to communicate, rather than conversing face to face or over the phone. When they do text, their words seem almost anonymous. It's much easier to say something rude in a text or post than directly to someone's face when you can see their reaction.

Have we changed so much that we are actually putting technology before humanity? I don't want to go all Socrates on you, but what is the real purpose of life? Isn't the essence and foundation of living really in the relationships we have? Go back to my funeral reference— don't we want to be remembered for being a good mother, a good husband, a good friend, someone who really made a difference in someone's life? We need to get off our devices and spend more time looking people in the eye and having real conversations.

Free Play

It's no surprise that with increased smartphone usage comes a decrease in outside play. Tech time up, outdoor time down. In fact, the time children spend playing freely outside is down a whopping 50 percent![37] It's almost hard to believe the change was so swift. It's a big loss for children, since outdoor free play is a perfect environment for kids to practice social skills with their peers in an unstructured environment. While playing outside with other kids, they learn invaluable lessons, exercise their empathy muscles, learn to think creatively and not just linearly, and get the added bonus of physical exercise.

Long days spent outside in free play have now been replaced by hours and hours of alone time on devices scrolling social media. Kids no longer feel the need to meet at the roller rink or pizza parlor since they are with their friends in virtual spaces, like the app Houseparty. Social media can clearly link kids together and make them feel like they have a lot of relationships—unfortunately, it can also make them feel left out, since teens are relentlessly detailing their hangouts on social media. This phenomenon isn't new, but checking Snapchat and Instagram and seeing what all your other friends are doing—without you—while sitting alone in your bedroom swiping away is very new. How can kids have hundreds of followers on their Instagram accounts and still feel like they don't have one real friend to hang out with on a Friday night?

I have always had "outdoor kids." We are lucky to live in a cul-de-sac that at one point had nineteen kids under age twelve. Our kids get home from school, eat a snack, and run out the door to play the game of the week—football, kickball, tag, hide and seek, basketball, jumping on a trampoline, sledding, snowball fights, or snow fort building. For a few summers, my son spent every free minute at our neighbors' house playing whiffle ball. Sometimes it would be just him and his buddy, and sometimes there would be ten kids. It didn't matter how many; they learned to negotiate the rules based on numbers, pick teams, keep score, and be the referees. If there were only three kids, one would pitch, one would hit, one would field. First base hit; they would put "Ghostie" on first, and the same boy would hit again. They would determine on the next hit how far "Ghostie" most likely made it to second or third base, etc. Talk about negotiation and imagination! This free play time and critical learning of social skills just cannot be replicated by staring at a screen.

> Tech time up, outdoor time down. In fact, the time children spend playing freely outside is down a whopping 50 percent!

Once inside, it was all about homework and board games. My family plays chess, Monopoly, Yahtzee, Trouble, Jenga, and every card game imaginable. We are from Wiskhaaaansin, the birthplace of Euchre and Sheepshead. (We have to be known for something other than cheese, beer, and the Packers, right? Scratch that, is there really anything better than the Green Bay Packers?) We have been in the same card club for fourteen years, but we're newbies compared to my in-laws, who have played Sheepshead with the same people over fifty years! At family gatherings, there is nothing better than a three-deck game of "Oh Heck" with fifteen people.

On those cold, minus 50-degree Minnesota winters, our kids would invent new games. Our daughter Belle invented a character affectionately named "Sock Boy." (This was when Belle was in the phase of wanting to wear two different colored socks—that was her thing.) She would take all her extra socks and tie them around her pre-schooler brother Greg, and he would run around the house as "Sock Boy," saving people from the bad guys (their stuffed animals). They made a video out of this which will definitely make an appearance at Greg's high school graduation party.

Bear with me—this Sock Boy story does serve a purpose other than to embarrass my children. You see, Sock Boy probably would have never been invented if my children were both tethered to their devices. They were bored and it was frigid outside, so the downtime allowed them to rise above the shallow and linear thinking often seen today and come up with a highly creative way to entertain themselves.

Let's take a quick rundown of a teen's day. They are in school around eight hours; sleep around eight hours; let's give two hours for personal grooming and eating. That is eighteen hours. Studies show the average teen is on a device seven hours a day. Yes, I'm a CPA—I know that math doesn't work and there aren't twenty-five hours in a day. As I said before, they are multitasking, eating and streaming, etc. With all their time demands in school and sleep, we must insist on downtime and free play to let the right side of their brains catch up with all the digital demands taking over the left side of their brains. And I truly believe my children would agree that non-tech time is a blast and is major bonding time for siblings.

Respect

To respect is to show an attitude of admiration, honor, or esteem.[38] Respect is a hard virtue to discuss because it has changed in so many ways, and its application to today's teens seems very fluid. For the baby boomer generation, there was a natural hierarchy that demanded our respect, and we gave it wholeheartedly. We respected our parents, our grandparents, our teachers, our doctors, our bosses, our coaches. We respected people based on title, position, wisdom, or age. There was a hierarchy in our communities and families, like a chain of command in the military.

I guess you could say this definition of respect really started to change when the baby busters chose to break away from the boomers after the explosion of MTV. Years later, millennials took this defiance of authority to a new level. There's been an entire generational shift now, and kids don't assume that just because someone is older they deserve respect.

When I had a question growing up, I could go one of three places: my parents, my teachers, or the *Encyclopedia Britannica*. Of course, the natural source for any child would be their parents, and with each touch point a stronger bond was formed. Consequently, our parents were admired and respected for all their advice and wisdom. When kids today have a question, they just ask Siri. It's shocking to think of how many conversations we are missing because our children can get faster answers to their questions from a search engine.

And kids are keenly aware that our knowledge of all the bells and whistles of smartphones pales in comparison to their almost instinctual navigation. They can run circles around us with almost every new digital product, feature, or app that debuts. My uncle sends me cute little quotes throughout the year, most of which are laugh-out-loud and spot on with generational differences. He recently sent this out: "I hate it when you can't figure out how to operate the iPad and the resident tech expert is asleep because he's five and it's past his bedtime." Having the child be an expert and the parent a novice is a new phenomenon, and we need to catch up.

For this generation of children and teens, adults have to earn respect. Parents are not just given respect because we are older; mothers are not admired simply because we carried them for nine months and spent forty-eight hours in labor. We earn their admiration and respect through our character, behavior, and knowledge, or whatever arbitrary measurement each individual child determines worthy of their respect. The sacrifices we make with our time, money, and sleep are just expected. As a parent of five children, I can tell you the bar for respect keeps moving and changing with each child's level of maturity, and most days it's hard to figure out what qualities they respect. The struggle is real!

As a baby boomer, I grew up with respect for elders, bound by lots of rules and restrictions. We operated in the narrow band of proper social conduct, and our job was to walk the line. Our compass pointed north, and clear lines were drawn between right and wrong. We took the concept of "fear of God" literally (even though it was mild in comparison to the Baltimore Catechism days of my parents, when nuns would slap you with a ruler for naughty behavior). The extent of our shenanigans in high school usually involved a park bench and a cheap bottle of TJ Swann. The drinking age was eighteen then; I was usually the designated driver.

On the other hand, growing up we had a huge amount of physical independence that would be unheard of today. Our parents weren't worried about our safety or whether we would get in trouble unsupervised. They knew everyone in town and were confident someone would help if things went awry. Our parents opened the door and said, "Go out and play, and come home for supper when the porch light comes on." If you were thirsty, you just ran into someone's yard and drank out of their garden hose. If you needed a ride, you hitchhiked. If you were late to get home and missed supper, they didn't save you a plate. You made yourself a PB&J sandwich.

Lots of my childhood freedom involved the Mississippi River. When I was in high school, my friends and I would just go out on someone's boat, park at a sandbar, and hang out. Our parents had

> Herein lies the contradiction in our parenting priorities: we micromanage where they are physically all day long, but are hands-off when it comes to the powerful computer in their hands that can cause damage in almost limitless ways.

absolutely no idea where we were or when we'd be back, but they didn't worry. They just assumed we were okay. We didn't have cell phones, so we couldn't check in even if we wanted to. We rarely crossed the line and broke their trust, so freedom prevailed. (There was a scary incident with an enormous barge, but no need to get into that now . . . what happens on the Mississippi stays on the Mississippi.)

In sharp contrast, millennials and Generation Z are being raised by the ultimate in helicopter parenting—nonstop cell phone connectivity and parents texting them and tracking their whereabouts throughout the day. To a certain extent, we are almost like their secretaries, managing their playdates, traveling sport schedules, piano lessons, homework, and orthodontist appointments. We are the ultimate smotherers and chauffeurs, driving them from one scheduled event to another. It's no wonder they have trouble seeing us as respected authority figures when we're doing mundane tasks for them all day long.

Herein lies the contradiction in our parenting priorities: we micromanage where they are physically all day long, but are hands-off when it comes to the powerful computer in their hands that can cause damage in almost limitless ways. They are never more than a few keystrokes away from all the filth you could possibly imagine. Am I the only one that finds this troubling?

Let's dive deeper into a couple of the role models we respected growing up versus the people our children appear to admire today. Teachers seem like a great place to start. Half the time I'm not sure kids are even listening to their teachers anymore, since so many schools allow devices in the classroom. And truthfully, compared to the graphic explosions and special effects they are used to seeing on their screens, I'm sure many teachers seem completely boring. If our kids have a question about Spanish, they can just use Google Translate; they don't have to wait until the morning to ask the teacher.

When we were picking a high school for our son last year, the extent to which devices were used in the classroom was a huge factor for us, and we did our due diligence. We chose a high school that had old-school textbooks, where kids took handwritten notes, wrote out notecards to study, used devices sparingly, and had no earbuds during class. Even with all that, our son gets plenty of time on screens doing research, typing lab reports, and writing papers.

With so many millennials entering the workforce, respect for the chain of command in the workplace is changing as well. In my career, I wouldn't dream of going into the CEO or CFO's office without making an appointment with his secretary. Leapfrogging the established chain of command would be disrespectful. Nowadays, millennials are breaking all the traditional boundaries in the business world. Like other millenials, our son Paul is completely comfortable doing "drive-bys," stopping in to chat with the CFO. In fact, it wouldn't be uncommon for them to actually "friend" their bosses on Facebook. While my generation would be appalled at their brazenness and impertinent attitude, a young CFO may even encourage them to do so. These changes are neither good nor bad, just very different from the respect model the older generation was raised on.

So who do today's kids really seem to respect and admire? Based on their social media activity, it seems their role models are Kim Kardashian, Justin Bieber, LeBron James, and Beyoncé—mostly sports stars, musicians, and a reality television star whose career was launched after a leaked sex video. Is this any surprise when some of our generation's most respected authority figures have let them down? Priests have been implicated in scandals, executives have been accused of sexual misconduct, sports heroes are arrested for domestic assault, and the President of the United States bickers with almost everyone, including his own staffers. It used to be Hollywood was fake, and news was real . . .

Respect can come in many different forms, not just the traditional, hierarchical model we used to see. Millennials bring independent thinking, entrepreneurial spirit, creative problem-solving, and their own unique ways of accomplishing unimaginable things. Like most millennials, one of our sons is liberal in most of his thinking, clothing, music choices, and political views compared to the conservative Midwest family that we are. He has sleeve tattoos, wears a beanie most days, and has a wardrobe composed mostly of black. But despite his outward, tough appearance, he has the biggest heart and passion for his career as a high school special education teacher. He can relate to those teens in ways neither I nor my husband could even comprehend. It is truly a calling, and for that he has earned our utmost admiration and respect—but only through years of us getting to know and appreciate his differences and understand that what makes him unique is really what makes him special. As parents of the next generation, we need to be open-minded, seek to understand their new ways of doing things, and respect many of the amazing changes that will make society better. That doesn't mean we have to lower our standards on respect—just broaden our definition.

> Teens today give as much credence to the person on the other end of their phone as the one sitting right across from them at a coffee shop or at dinner. Devices and people have near equal status.

I do, however, think we need to cling to some of the old standards for respect that seem all but extinct now. There is a pure lack of civility and manners displayed by all of us in this new digital era, from young to old. During a tour of Colonial Williamsburg, I read a list transcribed by George Washington in 1746, entitled "Rules of Civility and Decent Behavior in Company and Conversation." When we toured Mount Vernon, it was so obvious why George Washington was chosen as our first president and Founding Father. (I encourage everyone to do that trip—it's amazing!) The book has 110 simple rules of proper conduct. And what topped the list as number one?

1. *Every Action done in Company, ought to be done with Some Sign of Respect to those that are Present.*[39]

That's right: respect. Most of the rules are as applicable today as they were two hundred years ago, but many of them should really be applied now more than ever to our digital world, which clearly falls short of any semblance of high personal conduct. Let me give an example.

18. *Read no Letters, Books, or Papers in Company but when there is a Necessity for the doing of it you must leave.*[40]

Think about their time period, the eighteenth century. If you were having coffee with someone, you wouldn't just pull out the newspaper and start reading. Yet how many times do we check our email or social media when others are standing right in front of us today? Almost 90 percent of Americans took out their phone during their last social activity![41] There's even a new skill teens are working on called "eye contact while texting." Teens today give as much credence to the person on the other end of their phone as the one sitting right across from them at a coffee shop or at dinner. Devices and people have near equal status. Folks are even pulling out their phones and texting at funerals, corporate board meetings, and the movies, and don't even get me started on people who use their phones in a public restroom.

54. *Play not the Peacock, looking every where about you, to See if you be well Deck't.*[42]

Facebook and Instagram are like Christmas cards: we only show ourselves in the best light. They have become our families' highlight reel, not our blooper reel. We endlessly post every accomplishment of our children and fail to be truly vulnerable, posting about our kids having a temper tantrum, a fight with our husband, or when our child flubs the last play in the game.

65. *Speak not injurious Words.*[43]

How many things are posted on social media that you wouldn't dare say in front of a person, sign your name to, or show your parents or teachers?

I want to raise the bar on respect for others in this age of technology, both in person and on our screens. As parents, we need to train our kids to have good digital etiquette in this changing world of connectivity. More on that in my solution on digital citizenship, the Kindergarten lessons.

67. *Detract not from others.*[44]

If you were born prior to 1980, you know what an old-school phone booth is. Well, believe it or not, phone booths are making a big comeback, especially in office settings. More and more people are wearing headphones to drive out the noise of open cubicles; it's almost like they're putting up an invisible wall that says "don't disturb me."[45] Companies are installing phone booths with tables, chairs, and charging stations so you can use your cell phone in private and not disturb others.[46] This signals a gesture toward more civility: let's just be respectful of others and keep our private conversations private.

Humility

> "Humility is not thinking less of yourself;
> it is thinking of yourself less."[47]
>
> — Rick Warren, *The Purpose Driven Life*

The way I see it, humility is really a form of the virtue temperance, but I feel it's such an important topic in 2019 that it needs to stand alone in this book. In a world dominated by selfies, self-promotion, and self-branding, it's very timely to study this virtue. As far back as the eighteenth century, Benjamin Franklin listed humility as one of his thirteen virtues to aspire to, and it is no less relevant today than it was then.

> Kids who have come of age in the era of social media are trained not to have experiences but to record them.

The word "humility" grew from the Latin words *humilitās, humilis,* and *humus,* meaning "low" and "from the ground." One of the best teachers on this topic is Saint Thomas Aquinas, the Common Doctor. He's one of my favorites, since I went to high school at St. Thomas Aquinas—I had the amazing honor of being taught there in the 1980s by one of the greatest Catholic leaders of our time, His Eminence Cardinal Raymond Burke. St. Thomas Aquinas said, "*humilitās est veritas,*" which means "*humility is truth.*"[48] You are not seeing the world through your ego, you're in it. In other words, you are living in a state of humility if you are in touch with reality or grounded.

The classical worldview held pride as the opposite of humility. Think of it as the difference between having a conversation and being preoccupied with how the other person is perceiving you (pride) versus being lost in deep conversation and not trying the least bit to impress the other person (humility).

This is a challenge for teens today, since kids are so used to snapping pictures of everything that they often fail to really enjoy the event they are relentlessly trying to document. They are distanced from reality because they're always trying to play to an audience. There's a name for this phenomenon: "audience awareness." Kids who have come of age in the era of social media are trained not to have experiences but to record them. They have this strange need to tell others what they are doing all the time—looking at their experiences through the distorted lens of their cell phone camera.

No discussion on humility in this digital age is complete without a look at the 2013 *Oxford English Dictionary* Word of the Year, "selfie." Its use has increased 17,000 percent in one year and has 230 million hits on Google annually.[49] It's passé nowadays to ask a stranger to take a picture of you and your friends and just strike a pose. There is even "National Selfie Day," a Hallmark holiday for the digital age, which is June 21.[50] Is it just a coincidence that June 21 is also summer solstice, the longest day of the year? Natural lighting is important for good selfies! We are obsessed with taking our own pictures and sharing them. According to Rawhide, a nonprofit organization that assists at-risk youth, 74 percent of photos shared on Snapchat are selfies. In 2015, more people died by taking selfies than by shark attack. A common law of the internet is, "Pics or it didn't happen." And they need to make sure their audience "likes" their photos, since receiving zero "likes" would be interpreted as a social failure.

The actress Jamie Lee Curtis just wrote a cute children's book on this subject called *Me, Myselfie & I*. It cleverly tells a story of a mom who is given a smartphone and starts to become obsessed with selfies and documenting everything. The basic moral of the book is that the best things in life happen when the smartphone is turned off.

There's even a whole slew of products designed to make selfies easier to take—the most popular being the "selfie stick," one of *Time's* top twenty-five best inventions of 2014. Fast forward a couple years, and now the selfie stick is banned from many crowded venues like concerts since it is a nuisance to others. What's new on the horizon for 2018: a selfie drone designed by Zero Zero Robotics. This Hover Camera has a face and body tracker to literally follow you everywhere. It can take pictures of you from afar since you control it from your phone. Although the technology is amazing and creative, I'm sure it will be generating a lot of privacy and safety issues.

I grew up decades before anyone ever uttered the word "selfie." When I was a little girl, my first real experience with vanity and self-preoccupation came when I watched the Disney classic *Snow White and the Seven Dwarfs*. The wicked villainess in the movie utters the famous line, "Mirror, mirror on the wall, who is the fairest one of all?" Of course, back then, fair was synonymous with beautiful. At the time I watched the film, it seemed absurd to be so preoccupied with your appearance, constantly looking in a mirror. Fast forward to 2017, when Amazon rolled out their magic mirror–inspired technology called Echo Look. They describe it as a "style assistant" camera that helps rate your look based on "machine learning algorithms with advice from fashion specialists."[51]

Sure, growing up, we took pictures of our friends and family on our nifty Kodak box cameras. We patiently waited weeks for the film to be developed, then tossed the photos in a shoe box. But we wouldn't dream of turning the camera toward ourselves—that would have looked so absurd and narcissistic. However, with the invention of the smartphone quickly came the front-facing camera—originally intended to be used for video calling—the user was allowed to take pictures of themselves, and the modern selfie was born.

Selfies are not exactly new; self-portraits have been around for hundreds of years, just not in the form of digital media we have now. As far back as ancient Rome, Julius Caesar made sure to have his own face imprinted on the Roman coin.[52] Then came self-portraits using oil on canvas—a very time-intensive process, which is why so few have surfaced relative to the enormous number of digital photos. One of my personal favorites is found in Leonardo Davinci's *The Last Supper*, a replica of which hangs in my dining room. Rumor has it that Leonardo painted his own face as that of the apostle "Doubting" Thomas; a fitting display, since Leonardo was known to question everything and not take things at face value.

After oil paintings came box cameras, bringing with them the arduous task of getting the film developed. One of the first famous modern-day selfies was taken long before the internet even existed—in November 1966, astronaut Buzz Aldrin on Gemini 12 took a picture of his face in outer space, with Earth in the background. Now that was an amazing picture! And finally came the invention of the smartphone, its camera capabilities making selfies undeniably easy to create, delete, edit, share, and store.

Don't get me wrong—selfies are fun, and there is a place for them. What I am uneasy with is the pure infatuation people have with taking their own picture, and the means they go to to present the persona they want people to see. For the celebrities our kids are following on Instagram, it is not uncommon to take a hundred pictures before they get the perfect shot to post. Often it looks nothing like they look in real life, which sets many teenagers up to constantly be striving for a virtually unattainable look. And there are apps like Facetune that allow people to airbrush away their flaws for perfect skin, a perfect smile, and reshaped faces and bodies. I guess what it gets down to is that nowadays, kids seem to care much more about how they look than who they are.

René Descartes was a seventeenth-century philosopher who famously discussed the existence of life by reasoning: "I think, therefore I am."[53] I contend today's Generation Z (or should I say Generation ME), feels most alive and exhilarated when they are on their phones, almost as if their existence is validated by their social media activity.

I "snap," therefore I am . . .

I "like," therefore I am . . .

I "click," therefore I am . . .

I "post," therefore I am . . .

And this online existence can often contain a secret identity as kids exist across multiple platforms. For example, many teens have their "public" accounts that portray who they are to a larger audience, and a separate private account often nicknamed "Finsta" (fake Instagram), which can often be more real than the public account. In this underground digital world, teens feel free to confess their deepest and darkest secrets, often things most parents know nothing about. Tumblr is another site where teens share images and texts, many of which have dark and disturbing undertones.

One of the greatest modern-day examples of humility to me is Pope Francis. He is arguably the most beloved and popular religious leader since Pope John Paul II, and his humble nature and concern for the poor and oppressed have made him popular with folks of all faiths. Shockingly, even the supreme pontiff decided he had to join in on the discussion of smartphone usage! The Pope, speaking in November 2017 in St. Peter's Square in Rome, "said he was disappointed to see so many people using mobile devices when they should be worshipping during Mass." He said the priests who celebrate Mass ask the faithful to "Lift up your hearts" and not "Lift up your cell phones to take a photo! It's not only the faithful, but also many priests and bishops. Please! Mass is not a show!"[54]

This wasn't the first time Pope Francis had discussed this theme. Earlier in 2017, he asked, "What would happen if they checked the Bible as often as they checked their cell phones?"[55] In 2015, in his 192-page encyclical about climate change, the Pope warned of the dangers of bowing down to the altar of technology and putting a digital filter on our lives. "When media and the digital world become omnipresent, their influence can stop people from learning how to live wisely, to think deeply, and to love generously."[56]

When my family went sightseeing in Washington, DC, we took in the humbling and amazing experience of the changing of the guard at the Tomb of the Unknown Soldier in Arlington National Cemetery. The monument sits on top of a hill overlooking Washington, DC, and is dedicated to United States service members who have died without their remains being identified. My dad served in the Navy on the *USS Wisconsin* during the Korean War. He came back safely, and I have enormous respect and admiration for those serving our country. At Arlington, there is a ceremonial changing of the guard every half hour, complete with impeccably dressed soldiers, white gloves, and M-14 rifles.

Unfortunately, any amount of reverence or respect due the ceremony was overshadowed by almost everyone videotaping this event on their phone. I literally couldn't believe what I was seeing. To me, it was like filming the pallbearers carrying the casket at a funeral. We need to return to capturing events in our memories and really living them, not just filming them. Most things are available to view online anyway, if someone really wants to relive the experience.

So how do we get out of this self-absorbed mentality? It goes back to the quote I referenced at the beginning of the chapter: we need to think of ourselves less. I really believe the greatest form of humility is in service to others. Hopefully, by adopting some of my solutions in the last chapter, you can decrease your children's dependence on screens and help them to lead everyday lives of service and kindness.

We are passing the baton to this group of millennials and Generation Z's and entrusting the future of our nation to their hands. Many of our time-honored virtues are as relevant today as ever, and we need to be cognizant of ways to ensure their preservation in a digital land-scape. They need something to anchor to, and keeping these virtues alive will help ground them when technology continues to penetrate their lives at dizzying speeds.

"I want to live my life, not record it."

—Jacqueline Kennedy Onassis

Chapter V

The Solutions

I have given you all the data and all the research, and I have crunched the numbers (I am a CPA, after all). You know the statistics on how addicting and damaging screens can be for your growing child's brain, attention span, performance in school, and mental health. These are all compelling reasons to look closely at screen use in your home, and that may be all you need to motivate your family to initiate a radical change in behavior.

I did, however, miss one vital point as to why you should make some changes in your family's relationships with their devices. If you took the time to buy and read this book, your children's happiness is a top priority, and you take your parenting job seriously. I do as well, which is why this may come off sounding selfish: I admit it, I'm obsessed with my kids. I am all-in, and I want them to be as well. I want a real, deep, personal relationship with my children, and I don't want them to be distracted hiding behind a screen. I want to see what makes their eyes light up. I want to know what jokes they laugh at, who their friends are, what they're afraid of, what their passions are, who they are in love with, and what they want to be when they grow up. I get drunk on their smell, their laugh, their jokes, their talents. They're only little for a little while, and I want to really know them for this short period of time God has entrusted them to my daily care. I pray that deep connection during their childhood will carry us into a lifetime bond and commitment to each other. When we say no to devices, we're saying yes to each other. Keeping children away from their devices is denying them a relationship with an inanimate object and, in return, giving them the gifts of true, meaningful human relationships and love. Their phone costs a few hundred dollars; the gift of family is priceless.

Steve Jobs was famous for keeping things simple, which is pretty ironic considering he launched a very complicated age. All Apple stores look the same—white, with clean lines and no clutter. There are a lot of solutions in this chapter, and it would be overwhelming if you tried to enforce all of them, especially all at once. Let's keep this simple. Pick one solution, just one, and master that. Once you've conquered that one, move to another solution until that is mastered. Keep going until you feel your child has a healthy relationship with both the physical and digital world. Start simple, pick one, master that, move on . . .

If you have a newborn baby or young kids without devices, it should be easier to adopt many of these changes. If your kids are older and slightly addicted, involve them in the decisions. Let them pick the one to conquer first. When we explain the "why" behind our logic and involve them in the solutions, they are more likely to follow the new guidelines.

> Your relationship with your screen will speak louder than anything you could say to your kids.

Unfortunately, these guidelines probably won't make you very popular with your children. But this is one of the most important times where you don't want to keep up with the Joneses. Just because most eight-year-olds have a phone doesn't mean yours has to as well.

As I stated in my introduction, this book isn't just to build awareness of what screens are doing to our kids. It's a call to action, and your action items are listed in the rest of this book. Let's put some verbs in those sentences and make some progress! My solutions are grouped into the following categories:

- Sacred Space
- Sacred Time
- Monitor, Product, and App Solutions
- Unplug and Get Back to Reality
- Family House Culture

Let's get started making some changes!

SOLUTION 1

WTW (Walk the Walk). It starts with the parents. You have to model healthy screen use if you expect your kids to do the same.

Your relationship with your screen will speak louder than anything you could say to your kids. We can't tell our children to limit their time and then be on our own screens nonstop. Think of this as the flight attendant emergency notification: "If you are traveling with a small child who requires assistance, secure your mask first, then assist your child." This cannot be a "do as I say"—it must be a "do as I do." I'm sorry to say this, but oftentimes kids' screen use mimics their own parents' screen use. An addicted parent is usually a good indicator that their children will struggle with screens as well. We need to be good role models for our children in countless ways—eating healthy, telling the truth, caring for others—and screen use is right up there on the top. This is going to be an extreme challenge for parents who have adopted unhealthy screen habits. You need to let your children know you are changing your own screen habits based on new knowledge you've gained about screen time and its impact on health and happiness.

I know from having four kids already out of the house and living on their own that eighteen years go by in the blink of an eye. Often, when they get their driver's license is when they really start to pull away. You will have plenty of time to yourself once you are done with active, in-the-trenches daily parenting. These formative years are critical, so you just cannot let a screen raise your children. Millions and millions of parents before you got along just fine occupying their kids with no screens, you can too. It's vital we give our children our full, undivided attention. They need to know they are important and that what they say and do matters. By just listening, talking, and looking them in the eye, you will build a foundation of healthy self-esteem. Try counting up how many minutes you have face-to-face contact with your children versus how many minutes each of you are on your screen; it may be shocking and motivate you to make some changes. If you already limit your own screen time and your children's, good job! Keep it up.

Let me be clear: I'm not trying to blame or shame any parents reading this book. I know you love your children very much and understand this tech boom caught many off guard. Blaming doesn't solve problems, but taking action does. This book is a call to action! Before you start changing your children's use of their screen, make sure you feel your screen use is a positive example for them. Do the work, be the change you want to see in them, practice what you preach, walk the walk.

SACRED SPACE

Have physical boundaries between you and your phone

SOLUTION 2

Out of Sight, Out of Mind. Your phone is not a body part, so cut the cord. Keep it in a different room when you're not actively using it.

This is the most important lesson for you and your children. We talked about the similar addicting natures of screens, slot machines, and cigarettes. Every time we hear a ping, feel a vibration, or see the text bubbles pop up, we immediately get a dopamine hit and need more and more to feel satisfied. One way around this is to put some actual real estate

> Get that screen out of your eyesight and hearing range; proximity matters. If it takes actual effort to get to your phone, the work/reward ratio changes, and you're not as tempted to check it.

between you and your phone—create a physical barrier. Get that screen out of your eyesight and hearing range; proximity matters. If it takes actual effort to get to your phone, the work/reward ratio changes, and you're not as tempted to check it. If you're at home, don't carry it in your pocket everywhere you go. Set up a basket, box, or charging station and have everyone get in the habit of leaving their phones there, not on their physical bodies.

Make it a game with your kids, especially if they're showing signs of dependency. Set up challenges to see who can go the longest without touching their phone. Post the results someplace visible. Start small—say, fifteen minutes—then build from there.

SOLUTION 3

No Screens in Your Child's Bedroom. Period. Keep all cell phones, laptops, and computers out of bedrooms and only allow them in high-traffic areas of your home. This rule solves many of the problems discussed earlier—most of all, poor quality and quantity of sleep caused by late night surfing, temptation to sext and/or view pornography, and the EMF waves entering our children's brains through their relatively thin skull bones. Remember when I talked about the Silicon Valley executives limiting their own kids' use of technology? Some won't give their children phones until high school, and some won't allow data plans until they turn sixteen. The one rule that seems universally applied by these techies to their own children, regardless of age, is no screens in the bedroom. This is a dark hole you don't want to go down. Trust me, do not give in on this one.

One caveat: if you have a child heading off to college, there is no option for this solution, since all their belongings will be in their dorm room. Tell them not to sleep with the phone in their beds by explaining dopamine and all the other brain effects listed in this book. Have them keep the phone at least six feet from their head to minimize EMF exposure. Better yet, have them put their phone in airplane mode or turn it off. The alarm clock will still work in airplane mode. They can also put their phone in a "Blocsock" or "Faraday Bag" at night, which I discuss in the product solutions below.

Designate Sacred, Screen-Free Zones in Your Home. In addition to your child's bedroom, it's beneficial to establish sacred spaces in your home where devices are not allowed. We all need time and space to just relax, converse, hang out, and let our minds be quiet. Doesn't most creative energy really appear when our minds are free from all the clutter (remember the Sock Boy video)? That's why so many good ideas come to us in the shower, in bed, or on a phone-free walk. For our family, our children's phones never go upstairs to the bedroom level. That's the place they can go to just hang screen-free. You and your children have to decide where this is, then set up board games, bean bag chairs, a reading nook with books—whatever you want to promote as downtime without screens.

Do Not Carry Phone in Bra or Pants Pocket. Whenever a cell phone is turned on, its antenna is trying to stay connected with a nearby cell phone tower. In order to do this, it emits RF energy, even if you're not using it. The only exception is airplane mode, which turns off cellular data, Wi-Fi, and Bluetooth. "There's a significant drop-off in radiation exposure for every inch your phone is away from your body."[1] For girls, this is easier if they carry a purse. Most students carry a backpack, which is better than your child's pocket. Better yet, have your kids get in the habit of turning their phone off if they have to keep it in their pockets, then on again when they need to use it.

Use Your Laptop on a Table Rather than Your Lap. The individual who named the portable computer "laptop" should be fired! Given their name, it's pretty obvious people feel free to put laptops on their laps to work. That's not a safe bet for a couple of reasons. One is the proximity to the body and EMF exposure already discussed; two, having them on our lap forces us to look down, a big contributor to text neck and back pain. Remember the title to this book—#LookUp! An easy solution to this is to put your laptop on the table or desk, not on your lap.

Better yet, get a riser that moves the laptop closer to eye level so you don't strain your neck, especially with your desktop computer at home. Heck, prop it up on the old yellow pages for that matter—they're not used for anything anymore! Another great solution is to set up a workstation with a standing desk, which is adjustable and will get you out of your chair.

The book *Sitting Kills, Moving Heals* offers enlightening information about John Glenn and the astronaut program. In periods of weightlessness in space, astronauts, who are far fitter than the average adult, seem to rapidly age; their muscles, bones, and overall health degenerate to levels typically only seen in elderly people. The author found that keeping the subject resting and immobile, an extreme form of the typical American lifestyle, caused the same health problems as extended weightlessness. Let's get moving, not sitting around looking down on a screen.

Keep Your Cell Phone Away from Your Head. A cell phone sends out its strongest signal as it tries to connect during the first few seconds after you dial up a phone number. Most consumers don't read the fine print that comes with their cell phone, but the manufactures warn not to put your phone up to your head. It's especially bad to talk when you are in a moving vehicle, since your phone is bouncing from cell tower to cell tower. Some people are using Bluetooth or a headset, and that is better than having the phone right next to your head. Keep in mind, though, you are still being exposed to some radiation. Having your phone three feet away from your head reduces the radiation exposure by 90 percent.[2]

Use your speakerphone to talk when possible, at least when the phone is connecting to your call and the radiation surge is at its peak. I still have my old-school landline, and when I am making a long social call I use the landline so I don't even have to worry about the radiation. There are good deals available for landlines—my cable company threw in a home phone line for ninety-nine cents a month. Another good option is the air tube headset which I discuss below in product solutions.

> Having your phone three feet away from your head reduces the radiation exposure by 90 percent.

SOLUTION 8

Bathroom Etiquette: No Phones Allowed in Public Restrooms or Bathrooms at Home. Let's get back to keeping private activities private. No one wants to be using the facilities and hear you yapping on your phone or tapping away. That's just common sense and courteous bathroom etiquette. Have some respect for others taking care of their private bodily functions. In addition, many a phone has fallen right into the toilet and has been rushed to a bowl of dry rice. Just make it a habit and leave your phone out of the privy.

When you first buy your child a phone, tell them this rule and take their phone away for a day every time you catch them with it in the bathroom at home. If their phone does end up in the toilet, have them pay for the replacement. Back pockets are bad news. They need to own this one; you pick the behavior, you get the consequence.

SACRED TIME

Establish, nurture, and protect time without electronic devices

It's getting almost impossible for our kids to separate screen time from just . . . time. Today, 59 percent of adults say teens are too addicted, and it's time to get started on some practical ways to cut the ties.[3]

I know this section will be hard, but we have to keep in mind that we are their parents, not their friends. They will have plenty of friends throughout their lives, but only two parents. Setting reasonable time limits is not a punishment; you are really doing them a favor, trying to make the healthiest brain and body possible. We all have rules we have to follow: speed limits, city curfews, drunk driving laws, and work parameters. It's your job to set reasonable limits for their sleep time, play time, and homework time, and their screen time is no different. Give up the guilt, and they will thank you when they grow up.

I'm not going to sugarcoat this and pretend you won't have struggles with your child. You may have conflict every day in the beginning, but that doesn't mean you shouldn't do it. Screen use has to be viewed from a perspective of long-term happiness and health, not just what they want today.

I call this "Sacred Time" not to establish a religious connection but as something to identify as time you hold in high esteem, dear to your heart, deserving respect and reverence at all cost. Think of it as the time restraints that make your family unique and will differentiate you from other families. The Sacred Time recommendations fall into two main time categories: number of minutes per day with digital devices (duration), and time of day with digital devices.

> It's getting almost impossible for our kids to separate screen time from just . . . time.

This is going to be a huge undertaking, especially for parents who have come to rely on their kids' screens as virtual babysitters or entertainment so they don't have to. We can get this under control, but it's not just going to happen on its own; we need to have a plan and put in some real effort.

Let's go back to my food reference. If you want to eat healthy, someone is going to have to get in the kitchen—it's that simple. Screen time is no different—time to roll up our sleeves, put in some elbow grease, and tame the beast. Screen time choices need to be very conscious and intentional—not passive, not reactionary, and not lazy. We need to look at each request for the benefits of screen use and any unintended consequences, and then search for non-screen alternatives that would suffice. Not only are you saving your kids from being addicted to technology, but you're also saving them from other, more harmful addictions as adults. Remember, in the medical chapter we learned that 90 percent of addictions have roots in the teen years. Do you really want your child to have the odds stacked against him in adulthood and succumb to life-altering addictions such as alcohol, drugs, pornography, infidelity, overeating, or gambling? Hopefully this one fact alone will motivate you to take action. Now, on to sacred time solutions.

SOLUTION 9

The Cinderella Rule. Your phone has a curfew. All screens must be plugged into a central location by a certain time at night and left until morning.

We used to get into lots of fights with our oldest son over curfew. He didn't like our midnight rule, even though it actually was the law in our city for minors. We quit debating with him when we said, "Our car has a curfew." He was borrowing the family vehicle, and it needed to be in our garage at midnight or he lost the car for the next week. End of conflict. Boom.

Our children's phones need a curfew as well. They need to be put away for the night and not touched until the next day. For some, that will be ten o'clock; for others, seven. You decide. Phones are not your children's best friend, security blanket, or favorite stuffed animal. They are supercomputers in their pockets that are highly addictive. You determine where the central location/charging station is, but it shouldn't be in your children's bedrooms. I know parents who have to sleep with their kids' phones right next to their own bed or the kids will sneak out in the middle of the night and use them. Some of the monitoring products I discuss later can help you temporarily turn off their phone service (i.e. bedtime mode), or you can shut off Wi-Fi to the whole house. Some parents even change the Wi-Fi password every day so they can limit when their kids have service. For little kids, an easy way to limit is not to give them access to the phone charger. If they can't charge it, they can't use it.

SOLUTION 10

Shut Down Hour: Stop All Screen Activity One Hour Before Bedtime.

Kids need to turn their screens off an hour before they plan on going to bed so the blue light doesn't interfere with melatonin production. The Shut Down Hour can include things like making lunches, getting backpacks and clothes ready for the next day, brushing teeth, reading, and bathing. Once the Shut Down Hour begins, the phone should not be touched again until morning.

In order to accomplish this with older kids, we need to turn the homework model upside down. Screens have become almost a necessity for kids to get their homework done. I get it. Teach your children to do all their screen homework first. Have them get in the habit of handwriting a to-do list with everything that needs to get done and to prioritize screens first. Save the non-screen homework—reading, writing out math problems, art, and playing piano—for the end of the evening. Kids should have at least one hour of no screens before bed, and two is even better. Set the kitchen timer to count down if you have to.

 **Don't Touch Any Digital Device in the Middle of the Night.** This shouldn't be an issue, but better throw it out there. Don't you dare be that person that checks the phone after their middle-of-the-night potty break! This must be a problem area, since the new iOS 12 software update includes a customizable "do not disturb" feature to help those tempted to look at their phone in the middle of the night. It can be configured so your iPhone doesn't show you notifications if you look at the screen during certain hours. Be the opposite of Nike—just don't do it.

 **Turn Your Wi-Fi Off at Night.** Another great way to reduce your exposure to radiation coming from your internet connection is to turn your Wi-Fi off when you're not using it, especially at night. C'mon, you're sleeping anyway! Add it to the nightly routine of shutting the garage door, locking the front door, and turning the lights off. A lot of my friends have their Wi-Fi preprogrammed to turn off automatically at a certain time. Some tech gurus have even gone way old-school and returned to hardwiring their houses, another alternative to decrease wireless exposure.

 **No Screen Media before School.** I'm going back to my food references now. We all know that feeling of starting our day with a donut or pastry; it sets you up to spend the rest of the day craving sugar and unhealthy food. Screens are no different. When you wake up and touch your phone right away, it programs your whole day. Our cortisol levels are usually highest around eight in the morning for a reason—so that we are ready to face the challenges of the day. We learned earlier that screens increase cortisol levels, so we need to keep away from them when we first wake up to enjoy a calm, stress-free day.

Give kids a screen before school and they will start the day zoning out, making it harder for them to concentrate at school. Many teachers report being able to clearly tell which kids use screens before school and which do not. I know many of us are tempted to check our emails or read the news on our phones. Apple's solution is to roll out a new morning wakeup screen that's bare of notifications so you are "gently eased into your day." Seems much easier to just get in the habit of not touching it. Just like we have the Shut Down Hour at the end of the day, let's have a screen-free morning ritual as well. Make the conscious decision that your house will not start or end the day with screens.

SOLUTION 14

Only Check Your Email X Times Per Day. When I worked in public accounting, I would drag my audit bag home with me every Friday night. All weekend long, it loomed over my head, piles of audit workpapers lying within that leather bag. When I went most of the weekend without opening the bag, I had some serious Sunday night blues.

Now, we have created a work culture that makes us available almost 24-7 to our employers and friends. There's no such thing as family time and work time, since we are always available to work. Did you know that "70 percent of office emails are read within six seconds of arriving"?[4] The average worker checks their email thirty-six times per hour, keeping them always on high alert and constantly interrupted.[5] Our sense of priorities is distorted, as we now consider it urgent to read and respond to every email. Don't get me wrong—some of this is convenient and has allowed a certain amount of flexibility. But it's also virtually impossible to go off the grid for any extended period of time. More and more of a good thing isn't always good. I love the bold companies that are standing up for their employees' personal time and not allowing any emails after a certain time at night.

We need to teach our kids that home time is primarily family time and work can, and should, wait until morning and after the week-end. We can't be checking emails from the minute we wake up until we go to bed. Set up a schedule for checking email and stick to it. If you're really anxious, you can start with twenty-five times per hour. Take out one per hour until you can go an entire hour and build from there. Tell your kids so they can keep you accountable, and teach them to not check their own email once they have an account. Disable your notifications so you're not even tempted by the noise. Better yet, take your email account off your phone so it doesn't have to travel with you all the time, and only check emails on your desktop computer or laptop.

SOLUTION 15 **Take Away Your Child's Phone During Homework.** I've been using this rule since long before smartphones, when my children had flip phones with no data. Kids can't possibly concentrate on their assignments when they are texting and swiping every few minutes, constantly being interrupted.

If they need a computer for homework, have them use one in a common area and keep an eye on them in case they want to sneak their phone. They will be shocked at how productive they are without their phones and how quickly they can actually get their homework done when they're not constantly interrupted. Remember the study I referenced earlier—students who kept their phones on their desks had slower cognitive performance than students who had their devices in another location.

SOLUTION 16 **No Monkey Mind.** Prior to the invention of smartphones, if we really needed to get some work done, we would just close the door to shut away all the busyness and distraction going on in our home or office. Now, the busyness follows us everywhere we go. The most popular consumer product ever made—our cell phone—appears to be the biggest distraction in the history of mankind.

As we learned in chapter 3, there's no such thing as multitasking; it's really just switching tasks very rapidly, which is taxing on your brain. It also diminishes the virtue of empathy, since we're too distracted to step into another's shoes. We need to teach our kids to focus on one task or person at a time, and not to switch back and forth. We need to calm their monkey minds. I'm not talking about things like walking and chewing gum—I'm talking about using your memory, practicing cognitive decision-making, doing homework, driving, or concentrating on a conversation. You will be surprised at how your ability to perform a task goes up when you perform just the one task in front of you. Think of this as tapping into a whole new realm of brain power with extreme concentration and focus, a foreign concept to the multitasking generation.

One way to teach our children to focus on one thing at a time is the concept of mindfulness, or living actively in each moment. A basic method for mindfulness is to just slow down and observe how you breathe. Do this with your children; it will benefit the whole family. Before you start, turn off anything that dings, rings, pings, or could interrupt you. Take one deep breath through your nose and exhale through your mouth. Keep repeating, trying to just breathe for one minute. At first, your mind will wander—that's normal. Just get back to concentrating on the air in your nose or chest. Try to build up to ten minutes of deep breathing. Notice how you feel the rest of the day; it will keep you coming back for more. If you need a little more help on this one, there are literally hundreds of mindfulness and meditation apps available. Headspace has a free trial of a guided meditation, check it out and see what you think.

SOLUTION 17 **Limit Entertainment Media to X Minutes Per Day.** As I stated in "The Bennies" chapter, most kids are using their screens for four main purposes: entertainment (Netflix and other streaming services, gaming, social media), communication (texting, Facetime, Snapchat, phone calls), education (homework, college applications), and function (clock, camera, weather, shopping, GPS navigation).

While they might claim they are mainly doing homework on their phones and laptops, the data says otherwise. The majority are really wasting hours and hours on entertainment media. (*Fortnite!*) Over 70 percent of teens are spending three or more hours per day watching online videos.[6] After a day at school, transportation, eating, sleeping, and personal hygiene, you can do the math: there's not much time in here left for homework.

You need to rein in this entertainment media so kids have free time to connect with family, sleep, exercise, and enjoy downtime. You need to put clear and specific limits on the attention snatchers listed above so they don't exceed a maximum aggregate screen limit per day. This includes video games, Netflix, Facebook, Twitter, Snapchat, and other entertainment sites. Most of all, don't use screen time as a reward for good behavior. That will just make it seem more appealing and desirable to kids.

Set limits by age. The younger kids shouldn't have much screen time anyway. None of us are sure of the proper amount, but we definitely feel when it's too much. For school age, it really depends on whether they spend a lot of time on screens at school. Many parents insist on no digital entertainment during the week when the kids are already on devices at school. A big part of this will be building awareness so your kids actually understand how much time they are spending on each application. The monitoring software listed on page 126 will help you determine time used per application. Once you have actual usage, adjust to a healthy amount. Negotiate this with your older kids so they are part of the solution.

SOLUTION 18 **Set Daily Limits on Video Game Usage and Which Specific Video Games Your Child is Allowed to Play.** Video games can be both educational and fun, and many of the designers are downright brilliant. Playing video games in moderation has unique advantages: they promote problem-solving and creativity, make it easier to bond with friends who see gaming as a social activity, teach skills such as strategy and cooperation, and foster healthy competition. They can be played alone, with friends, or with parents. Video gaming can be perfectly fine if the content is age appropriate and reasonable time limits are enforced.

On the other hand, video games can also be very addicting, and violent games can desensitize our children. We must take an active role in deciding which games our children can play and for how long. As with most parenting choices, it's imperative that you do your research and are armed with the right information. The rule in our house is no violent games and a thirty-minute daily limit on games we've preapproved. On most days, my kids have been too busy with other things to even think about video games unless they had a sleepover, and even then they mainly pick sports games such as football or basketball.

The first thing you want to do is learn how to use your console's parental controls. They all have them. Do a tutorial and set them up right out of the box. The next thing you want to consider is what the game your child wants is rated. Just like movies, all video games carry a rating. Video games ratings are assigned by the Entertainment Software Rating Board (ESRB), and full information on the rating system is easily found online.[7] If you wouldn't let your child go to an R-rated movie, they shouldn't be playing video games rated "M" for mature. The website www.pluggedin.com is also a great resource for video game reviews (and movies, television shows, music, apps). They go much deeper into content than the straight entertainment ratings for good media discernment.

Other parameters to consider with video games:

- Determine which games your children can play in your house and apply the same rules for when they are at a friend's house. Speak to friends' parents and make it clear your child isn't allowed to play certain games. If no parent will be home, don't let younger kids even go over there.

- Preview the game before allowing your children to play it.

- Be aware, some games let children play with and talk to anyone in the world. This may expose them to harsh language, bullying, stalking, or harassment. We know that not everyone online is who they say they are, but sometimes children have trouble realizing this. If you do allow them to play online, ask who they are playing with, sit in on some games, and listen to the language. At a bare minimum, tell your children to never give out personal details like their name or address online.

- Set the rules around in-game purchases, if any are allowed.

- For young kids, change the setting on their device to "airplane" mode. That way they can only play the game offline and won't accidentally make gaming purchases or connections with strangers.

- Predetermine how long they can play. Give them a five-minute warning before time is up so they can save their game.

- Use monitoring software to determine how much time children are playing in aggregate on all devices, including their phone, iPad, and Xbox. Take into account other screen activity such as streaming videos and homework. If they are addicted, start small, scaling back their time limit each week until they have a healthier relationship with gaming. If needed, there are video gaming addiction camps your teen can attend if you feel your home program isn't working.

SOLUTION 19

Never Pull Your Phone Out at a Red Light While Driving. I find this habit infuriating, especially since there are laws against it. We've all been behind someone at a red light who doesn't notice that the light has turned green. (You know who you are). It's like this absolutely urgent message magically appeared and they had to bridge the few seconds of downtime between the red light and green light with something.

Every time you check your phone while driving, you are forging new neural pathways that turn this routine more and more into a habit.

Is it really that important to see what you missed while driving? Is

> Research indicates drivers using hands-free phones only see half of the information in their driving environment. This phenomenon is called "inattention blindness."

it worth risking an accident? Can you really not cope with a few seconds of boredom? What example are you setting for the future drivers in the car? This is a bad habit, and we need to just cut it out. Each time you resist the urge, it will get easier and easier to refrain and just concentrate on the road.

SOLUTION 20

It Can Wait, Don't Text and Drive. In the multitasking chapter, we talked about distracted driving. We have to get the message through to our teens that *texting while driving is six times more likely to cause an accident than driving drunk!*[8] Why is there such a stigma attached to drunk driving and not texting while driving? Despite the laws in place, this is still an epidemic, and to me it's scary to see teens and even middle-aged people on their phones when they're driving.

You may think my solution to this is to use a hands-free device. Wrong! It may seem counter-intuitive, but research shows that hands-free does not eliminate the cognitive distraction and is still unsafe. In a National Safety Council poll, 80 percent of respondents said they believe hands-free devices are safer than handheld, and 53 percent said they believe voice control features are safe.[9] However, research indicates drivers using hands-free phones only see half of the information in their driving environment.[10] This phenomenon is called "inattention blindness" and can lead to drivers missing items such as stop signs and pedestrians. Do we really want our teens only seeing half of what's before them? They already struggle with making good decisions, since the all-important frontal lobe of their brain isn't fully developed. We don't need to add to this.

First and foremost, have your teen give their word they will not use their phone while driving. I have my children put their phone in the trunk of the car so they're not tempted to pick it up—as long as it's nearby, it will be screaming their name.

If you don't trust your teen to keep their word, you can go one step further; you can block all cell service to their car. They can still call 911, and certain phone numbers can get through if you'd like (yours, for example). The app that will do this blocking for you is listed below under product solutions on page 131. At a minimum, look for a "do not disturb while driving" setting on their phones, with which their phones will detect when they're moving and will automatically silence incoming alerts and notifications. If a phone doesn't have this setting, you can download the AT&T DriveMode app. The app will turn on automatically when you're driving fifteen miles per hour or faster, and turns off shortly after you stop. You don't have to be an AT&T customer to use the app. Parents can even receive a text message if the app is turned off or if other safety features are disabled.

Along with giving their word, have your kids pledge not to drive distracted. The NHTSA has launched a campaign called "It Can Wait," urging drivers to resist the urge to text from behind the wheel. Have all drivers in your household take the pledge, including parents, and hold each other accountable. The pledge can be found at ItCanWait.com—more than thirty-two million pledges have already been made.[11]

There's a reason my first recommendation is to have your child give their word they won't be on their phone while driving. We need to help build their character, and keeping their promise to you is a big part of this. In my opinion, a sign of a truly good character is not what you do in front of people but what you do when no one is looking. The data for texting and driving support this. The NHTSA say that only 36 percent of drivers will look at their smartphone if there is a passenger in the car, even fewer if the passenger is a child. However, 64 percent will look if they are alone. Even better, tell your friends not to do it, since 78 percent of teen drivers say they won't text and drive if their friends tell them it's wrong.[12] You have to teach your kids so they can tell their friends. Even when you're driving, walk the walk!

Don't Text and Walk. Let's take this one step further. In the medical chapter, I talked about the sidewalk in China with walking lanes and walking-while-texting lanes. But these problems of distracted walking exist worldwide. Since the death of a fifteen-year-old girl in Munich who was hit by a tram while looking down at her cell phone, anti–distracted walking measures have been popping up in Germany, including embedding traffic lights right in the pavement so pedestrians can see changing lights even while looking down.[13] Do we really need to stoop—no pun intended—to this level?

Some brave CEOs are taking steps to ban cell phones from the workplace, at least during meetings. Mat Ishbia, CEO of United Wholesale Mortgage, recently asked that his executive team and other managers not check their phones as they walk to and from meetings. "Don't act like we're too important to say hello," he told them. "Make eye contact with people."[14]

You taught your children not to run with scissors—now teach them not to walk and text.

No Screens on Short Car Rides Around Town. I have been part of car-pools for over twenty-five years, since our kids have been in every extracurricular activity available (soccer, Scouts, football, basketball, piano, trumpet, dance, swimming, musical theater, speech, robotics, math league, track, cross country, and volleyball, to name a few). It's no surprise that by the time I traded in my minivan, I'd racked up 220,000 miles driving my kids around. I loved those days!

My oldest son is now twenty-nine years old, and my youngest is fifteen. Years ago, when my oldest and his friends would pile in the van, it was always incredibly loud. One story after another, rehashing practice, laughing, joking—such great bonding time. Now, when I give rides to my iGen youngest child and his friends, as soon as the butts hit the seats, the phones are out and the earbuds are in. Silence. (That is, unless they are playing each other in a video game on their phones and utter comments on the match.) Maybe it's the dynamics of his class, maybe they're uncomfortable talking in front of me, maybe he hangs with a shy group—who knows. I am happy to do it and not judging; it's just very different.

Is it really necessary for kids to be on their phones for every car ride they're with you? Maybe it's fine on long road trips to make the hours go faster, or when kids are uncomfortable talking with the other passengers, but during a simple, fifteen-minute jaunt around town with you, they shouldn't be needed. Save them for times when there are not many good alternatives, like when you're stuck on an airplane. Start this young; keep things in the car to occupy them, like books or snacks. Better yet, play car games: slug bug, the ABC game, the license plate game, "ghost," wave to semi drivers—you get the drift. Best of all, you have a captive audience—use it and talk to your children.

A key reason for this limitation besides the obvious screen time limit is that the metal parts of your car magnify radiation; your phone has to work extra hard to increase its transmitting strength as you travel between cell towers. Our kids' growing brains don't need this. If they are on their phones for short car rides, make sure this time is part of their daily screen limit. We need to challenge this one hard; when they are driving, we don't want them to associate being in a car with having their phone out. We need them to associate the car with a phone-free zone.

SOLUTION 23

Establish "24-7 Digital Fast" Days.
Go twenty-four hours without your devices, seven times a year, parents and kids alike. The best days to try this are during the summer, school holidays, weekends, and vacations. Since I am Catholic, I have to throw out the idea of a forty-day Lenten fast from screens. Think of it as a sabbatical for your eyes, ears, fingers, and most of all, brain!

Did you know the word "breakfast" was actually first applied when people would break their fast of not eating for an extended period of time? St. Thomas Aquinas, in his *Summa Theologica*, lists eating too soon as one of the ways to commit the sin of gluttony. In medieval times, fasting was seen as evidence of one's ability to negate the desires of the flesh; the ideal eating schedule was a light midday meal followed by heartier supper in the evening. I have researched intermittent fasting extensively for my own personal regime, and I think the key Thomas Aquinas was getting at was timeboxing eating into a shorter window—say six or eight hours a day—which means either breakfast or dinner is a lighter meal or none at all.

I think a similar healthy concept can be a fast not for our stomachs and digestive systems but for our eyes, ears, and fingers: putting down our screens. We need to get rid of this continual racket and take a conscious step to quiet our mind. Start with a full day, and build up to a whole weekend if you can. There are even camps where kids go for weeks without touching a device. What a luxury to go off the grid for that long! We have a home phone so we can still call, but you may need to keep one device on for emergencies. We recently had a ten-day family trip where none of our phones had service; it was heaven. We just enjoyed each other's company, and no one was preoccupied with their phone. Trust me—you can do this.

I interviewed a parent who had tried the concept of a digital fast with her eighth-grade child. He was becoming withdrawn, angry with family members, and spent a lot of time in his room or with friends but not much in the common family area. His parents had tried limiting his screen time usage and location but found them difficult to monitor, especially when he was with friends. The parents decided to ground him from all electronics for one week. The first day, he was angry and "hated" the whole family. On day two, he spoke mainly in short, grumpy sentences. By day three, he had asked to play cards with his mother. On day four, he was joking and talking with the family members nonstop. His mom says she truly believes she witnessed him "detoxing" his brain and he started acting like a normal thirteen-year-old boy again once the electronics were banned.

I applaud her tenacity to stick with a week-long digital fast, and have read studies that confirm children can show improvements in just a five-day digital fast. Maybe you can try this with your own children at times throughout the year.

SOLUTION 24 **No Screens at Mealtime When Others Are Present.** This includes meals at home and restaurants. If there are people present, put the phone away.

This recommendation is a salute to George Washington's "Rules of Civility."[15] Just because it's not the eighteenth century doesn't mean we can't maintain a certain level of civility when in the company of

Family mealtime is a sacred tradition that we have to nurture and keep alive.

others. I cannot count how many times I've been at a restaurant and have seen two parents and two children, all four looking down at some kind of device, completely ignoring each other.

When you are with people at a social gathering, please do not be on your phone. Don't even have it out, because you will be tempted to check it. Just enjoy the face-to-face contact and company. Give your attention to actual, live human beings sitting with you, not an inanimate object. It's also courteous to the wait staff to not be on our devices, and there will be future work settings where you cannot get in the habit of ignoring coworkers in favor of your device. I saw a cute ad that said, "Putting your phone away and paying attention to those talking to you? There's an app for that, it's called RESPECT."

Study after study shows how important it is to have family mealtime to catch up with our children on their days, their friends, and their schooling. We need to dedicate our undivided attention to this time, and we can't do this if we're staring at a screen. If your phone pings in the middle of dinner, ignore it so you can teach your children how to act when they are with their friends. If you're a family more on the introverted side and not big on conversation, that's fine; play a game during dinner. "Family Feud" is fun and can pass the time with many laughs; you can also just bring a deck of cards to pull out when you're at a restaurant. There are a ton of conversation-starter games out there—just pick one up.

Family mealtime is a sacred tradition that we have to nurture and keep alive. I'm at the tail end of raising my children, and believe me, I would do anything to have all of us sitting at our dinner table again every night. Each time another child goes off to college, there's a mourning period at dinner with an empty chair. I know that's God's plan, and they need to be independent. Just treasure those moments—they go by so quickly. Before we know it, those chairs will be filled with adult children, their spouses, and grandchildren, if we're lucky. In fact, just last week our daughter blessed us with our first grandchild! Those traditions of family bonding over meals—away from screens—need to be established when they're young if we have any hope of them sticking when they go off into the real world.

Have your heard of a phone stack? Some teens are starting to put their phones in the middle of the table at restaurants so they're not distracted and can enjoy each other's company. First one to give in and touch their phone pays the bill. I don't know many teens who could afford to pay for all, but I love that they recognize the distraction and have found a clever solution. Great idea—an even better enhancement would be to put the phones out of sight so they're not screaming your name. You can still have the rule that whoever touches their phone pays—just don't leave them visible.

Notice my solution reads "when others are present." I see nothing wrong with eating alone and using that time to catch up on emails or connect with others virtually. When you're alone, you are not being rude to anyone by ignoring them. Just be careful to not adopt the habit of mindless eating and scrolling—you need to stay healthy.

SOLUTION 25 **Put Your Phone Away When You Are Paying.** One of my old bosses taught me a great lesson about always being on time when I was younger. He said that when you arrive late to a social or business meeting, you send the message to the other person that their time is not valuable— whatever you were doing that caused you to be late was more important than what they may have had going on themselves. Being on time shows that you respect the other person. That really stuck with me, and I am rarely ever late thanks to this advice.

I think the same applies when we are paying at retail establishments. It's just rude to be on your phone when someone is serving you— doesn't matter if it's the teen at your local coffee shop, the cashier at the grocery store, or the waiter trying to take your order or hand you your check. (I would say the banker at the teller window, but millennials wouldn't even know what that means.) Whenever you're interacting with someone behind a counter or at a register while making a transaction, give them your time, attention, and—most of all—gratitude for helping you. These hard-working Americans are often grossly underpaid. Please treat them, and others, with dignity and respect.

SOLUTION 26

Let Your Kids "Get Good and Bored"!

Recently, I listened to an interesting Katie Couric interview; her guest was Jeane Twenge, professor of psychology at San Diego State University, author of *iGen*, public speaker, and consultant. Her research centers on differences between generations, specifically the alarming increase in mental illness among today's youth, much of which she attributes to social media and screen use. She doesn't allow her kids to have phones, and they have limited use of her tablet. One comment from Dr. Twenge stood out: "Do kids today say 'I'm bored' anymore?"

> We need to create times of delayed gratification to counteract the quick wins coming from their devices.

How many times did our parents hear that when we were young? Usually parents responded with a list of chores a mile long to occupy us, unless we were on long car rides—then they had to play car games with us or we'd continue to jab and poke at our siblings until we drove them crazy! Today, our children aren't constantly nagging us saying they're bored, since kids have 24-7 access to their devices. Dr. Twenge had great advice to parents in her podcast: let your kids get good and bored.

I love that line. I think this solution is a great response to today's instant-gratification culture. Some kids act like their phones give off life-giving oxygen, and go into a full-blown panic if they're without them. We need to teach them it's okay to be without their phones, without constant entertainment. It's okay to patiently wait for what you want. We need to create times of delayed gratification to counteract the quick wins coming from their devices. These are skills necessary to build the virtues of temperance and self-control essential for a happy, successful life. Research shows that strong self-control is a

> It's during the downtime that our "brains process and consolidate information."

predictor of success and happiness.[16]

Kids are so busy with school and extracurricular activities that often-times they forfeit downtime to be on their devices. We live in this lie that we have to endlessly be producing or entertained. As parents, we're so busy writing down our "to do" lists that sometimes we forget it's just as important to not do anything at all. We have to realize unplugging is not a luxury—it is a necessity. There is a medical reason for this; we do most of our thinking when our brains are idle! Yes, read that again. It's during the downtime that our "brains process and consolidate information."[17] *Research on naps, meditation, nature walks, and the habits of exceptional artists and athletes reveals how mental breaks increase productivity, replenish attention, solidify memories, and encourage creativity.*[18] So, the next time you're wondering why your kids can't remember all the words for their spelling test, turn off the digital world, indulge in the real world, and let them get good and bored.

Some people are so passionate about bringing more downtime into our day that they have joined grassroots movements to ban pulling your cell phone out in public. They want to draw clear boundaries, as with smoking, about where it is socially acceptable to use a smartphone and where it isn't. Maybe that's too far, but I recommend building boredom into your day.

Even the cell phone giants are starting to recognize that kids aren't getting needed downtime. A new Apple release that came out this fall is called "Downtime." This option will allow parents to limit kids' app usage by category. Critical apps will still work, like making phone calls, but notifications will not be displayed and a badge will appear letting kids know certain apps can't currently be used. That's a step in the right direction, but I think downtime with no device is better.

There is a thirteen-year gap between my oldest son and my youngest son. Given how busy all my kids have been through the years, we called our little guy our tag-along baby, Ready Freddy, since we were always on the move. He turned out to be the biggest fan our kids had ever known, alongside their grandpa. Now that he has his own activities, the tables are turned. The big kids are busy going to college, falling in love, and starting their careers, but they all make time to be his cheerleaders at his events. Sure, they could be at home streaming movies. Sure, it's boring sitting through game after game, inning after inning. But they do it anyway because they want him to know they're in his corner. We need to bring our kids to physically cheer their siblings on and not give them a device to occupy them. Our children need to know they are each other's biggest fans, even when it's cold, rainy, snowy, and yes, boring! You never know when you're going to get the chance to pitch and win the State Metro baseball league championship under the lights at 11:00 p.m. at the Kent Hrbek Field, but you will always remember who was there to cheer you on.

Screen time needs to be intentional and purposeful; don't use it as the default when your kids are bored. Help them separate true needs from wants. Start small and gradually increase the waiting time between what they want and what they get. You can give them guidance on fun, relaxing, screen-free, brain-saving activities. Have them write down ten of their favorite non-screen activities and pull that list out when they say they're bored without their phones. For some kids, it might be going for a walk, meditating or praying, having a cup of hot chocolate, writing in a journal, playing with legos, crafting, or reading. It is also important that kids learn monotonous chores, since many of their early workdays will include boring, repetitious, mindless tasks. Have them wash the windows, change bedsheets, put away clean dishes, weed the garden, clean their bedroom, set the kitchen table, fold laundry, and go grocery shopping with you.

MONITOR, PRODUCT, AND APP SOLUTIONS

SOLUTION 27

Solution 27: Establish a Baseline Media Usage. A good starting point to gauge where your kids depend on technology is to quantify the problem and figure out exactly what you're dealing with. This is one scenario where we can harness the positives of technology to get a handle on the situation at hand. Information is power, and we can't very well have discussions on appropriate content and time limits when we have no idea how much our child is even using. Think of this like money management—you can't figure out a budget if you have no idea how much you're spending for food, rent, and utilities.

Use a monitoring service to build awareness of your child's daily habits and get a baseline usage, and build from there. When you start out, have your child write down how much they think they are using each app; chances are the monitoring software will show much higher usage. After you monitor, establish a baseline, and set the child's daily limits, if all is running smoothly you can cease monitoring, or use it as extra insurance if you have a child who is not as trustworthy.

In addition, while tech has made it easier to connect and our kids are physically safer, it's much harder to keep our kids safe from dangers in the virtual world. We need tools to set parameters for appropriate content for each child's age and maturity. In order to make good decisions, we need to do our homework, invest some time in monitoring actual usage, and go from there. My guess is your kids are racking up more hours than you ever imagined. A recent study said we touch our phones 80 times a day[19] and millenials touch theirs 150 times per day.[20]

There is a broad spectrum of monitoring capabilities out there, and you have to consider the functionality and decide which is best for your family. There's a fine line between using information to make good decisions and spying on your almost-adult children. Will you only look at time usage? Will you block pornographic sites? Should you see which websites your child is clicking on? How about reading all their texts? I want to give you a place to start moving in the right direction. The ability to monitor devices falls into the following main categories, all with corresponding daily and weekly reporting capabilities:

- Total minutes on device per day/week
- Number of times phone or device touched in a day
- Minutes spent on each app
- Number of text messages sent
- Websites visited
- Copies of text messages, pictures, social media messages sent
- Location of device/child
- Driving applications—speed of vehicle, fast braking, location, texting while driving, and more

How do we go about starting to monitor? When you first get your child a phone, iPad, or computer, make sure you set up the proper parental controls, filters, and firewall to restrict access to inappropriate content, especially "adult" websites. Also, if you agree on a new app or game to download, play it with your child so you know exactly what it does. For example, most parents think Snapchat is a harmless social media app that lets you send quick pictures to your friends. Yes, it does have that feature. However, swipe to the Discover tab on Snapchat, and you are instantly given access to a plethora of news and clickbait features totally inappropriate for minors. Here are some recent headlines: "People share their secret rules for sex," "Rita's nude vacation snap," "People tell us their weirdest stoner snacks." A great source of information is a website called Common Sense Media, which can help you determine if a program, game, or app is appropriate.

Once the device is set up, there are three main ways to monitor usage— through your service provider, through third-party software, or, for newer phones, through the device itself. I am most impressed with the new "Screen Time" app that was released in October 2018 and came free with the new iOS update. Finally, the phone manufacturers are starting to give parents easy ways to combat device addiction! I urge you, if you haven't already, make sure all your children's devices have Screen Time and you monitor the activity. You can see how much time they are on their device, how many times they pick up their phone, which apps are used, for how long, and how many notifications are received; set time limits by day; and lock the child out of their device at bedtime. All are great enhancements and a step in the right direction.

There are also dozens of third-party software monitoring packages; you really need to do your homework and pick the one best for your family. We have Disney's "Circle" and are very pleased with its functionality and ease of use. Every day I can set time limits for my son's use of apps like Instagram and Twitter. I get notified if he downloads a new app, I can tell how long he's been on his phone, and I can set his device to "bedtime" mode to turn it off temporarily. We also have Life360, which tracks his location, on his device. This has been especially helpful when he loses his phone and we can see exactly where it is!

Some other apps, which can help with everything from monitoring how often a phone is checked to making sure pornography isn't accessed, include Moment, Checky, Kidslox, Unglued, Covenant Eyes, Luma, and OurPact. Probably the most restrictive I've seen is called "MyMobileWatchdog." With this service, you basically receive the same messages as your child, be they texts, pictures, emails, or phone calls. This seems very intrusive, but if it is in response to major behavioral and trust issues, it may be an option for some families.

Keep in mind, no monitoring service will be 100 percent reliable— kids can be sneaky if they really want to. Another limitation: if their phone is off, you can't track their location. When you get to developing your family media plan, you can set the parameters and consequences for when they fall short of your expectations.

SOLUTION 28

Wear Felix Grey Glasses When Using Screens at Night. As discussed in the medical chapter, screens are wreaking havoc on our eyes and causing a whole myriad of symptoms including eye strain, eye fatigue, headaches, itchy eyes, and blurred vision. The Vision Council reports that 200 million Americans have some of these symptoms.[21] The four main causes are blue light, glare from screens, close-up viewing, and being so absorbed in our screens we forget to blink. Think about it: computers and screens have only recently been developed, and our eyes have not evolved to close screen use and blue light. Who knows if they ever will—or if we even want them to.

The obvious cure is to just get off our screens, but that's not always feasible given the major portion of our productivity that depends on computer use. If you have to stare at a screen for your employment or school homework, the most widely recommended first defense to protect your eyes is the **20-20-20 rule**. Every 20 minutes, look away from your screen and stare at something 20 feet away for 20 seconds. This will reduce stress on your eyes. Eye drops and artificial tears can also temporarily help.

One of the best solutions I've seen comes courtesy of my daughter, who is in medical school—it is called Felix Gray glasses. These glasses have lenses specially designed to mitigate strain on the eye when using screens. My daughter and most of her medical school friends have them, as they are often studying online into the wee hours of the night. The glasses come in prescription, non-prescription, and reader's varieties. The name-brand version is around a hundred dollars, but there are literally dozens of knock-offs available—a quick Amazon search will show what's out there. The reviews show that most of the cheaper versions may be inferior because they distort colors toward yellow, cause dizziness and nausea, and look unattractive. If you look at the Felix Grey website, you'll see these glasses are worn in the offices of Amazon, Google, Spotify, Apple, Facebook, and Goldman Sachs. Another hack from the Silicon Valley techies!

SOLUTION 29

Go "Old School." Or "vintage," as the young kids are saying. Just because almost every consumer product out there seems to come with a "smart" model, do we really have to buy them? Sometimes the smarter thing to do is just dumb it down. Instead of hearing "smart" as a positive, we should instantly associate smart with "constantly searching for internet service." Do you really want all those EMF waves going through everything in your house and into your children's growing brains? We can give up some of this connectivity and not lose any functionality; we just have to challenge the status quo. Let me give some examples.

For research on this book, I had some friends try Moment, an application that shows how many times a day you touch your phone. The new Apple update actually includes this same functionality, so make sure you use it. Many thought they exaggerated when they estimated they picked up their phone fifty times a day, when in reality it was triple or quadruple that amount. One common theme came out loud and clear: they were using their phones to check the time. Why not just wear a watch and decrease that dopamine hit from wanting to touch your phone? Easy peasy.

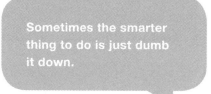

Sometimes the smarter thing to do is just dumb it down.

Speaking of time, how about our daily calendars? I am one of those moms who always has the old-school, hard-copy, month-by-month calendar on my wall. It has each family member's handwritten schedule. I tape it up for the month and have a full year's calendar handy. All the kids know to check it at night before they go to bed and add anything new to the calendar. Training my husband in this has been a challenge, I'm not going to lie . . .

I know many smart and accomplished moms who take this handwritten calendar a step further and color code for each family member. I'm just not that crafty. I've had this conversation with other, younger moms who brag about the electronic calendar on their smartphone that is synced with other family members. They say my idea is not practical since they may be at the orthodontist, need to make an appointment, and not know their calendar since it's at home. But it's very rare that I encounter that situation, and just in case I periodically take a picture of the calendar with my phone so I can reference the photo. And guess what? I can always just call the doctor and make an appointment when I get home. These are little changes that have crept into our lives that are really forcing our kids to keep touching their phones. It's just not essential when there are non-screen alternatives. Another added benefit—if one of our older kids needs to call me to check what's on the calendar at a future date, they usually stay on the phone and get me all caught up on their week. Touch points, people, keep them open.

Another old-school time fix: how to wake up in the morning. No, I'm not going old-school enough to suggest you get a rooster—although that would be fun—just a basic, ten-dollar alarm clock for everyone's bedroom. Let your kids pick out their own so they buy into the idea. Kids don't need to sleep with their phones just so their phones can wake them up. Train everyone to use the alarm clock to decrease touching your phone as soon as you wake up, as well as to avoid EMF hitting you all night long. Instilling this while your children are young is crucial so that when they head off to college, they're not sleeping with their phone next to their head in bed—don't need any more pillow fires out there! I know I may sound like June Cleaver from the *Leave it to Beaver* days, but this is just an easy way to decrease our dependence without having our quality of life suffer. Think functionality without screens when available.

Another big one: your child's wireless baby monitor. We don't need that constantly searching for a signal when your baby's skull is so thin and fragile. Just get a hardwired monitor. Or, if you're us and long on kids but short on bedrooms, put the crib in your bedroom—no monitor needed. I can honestly say I miss the time when our little guy slept in the crib next to us. Those days were precious.

For that matter, I dare you to resist buying all the new "smart" appliances and thermostats that depend on having a wireless signal. Since they constantly need a Wi-Fi signal to operate, you cannot really shut off the Wi-Fi at night to decrease EMF exposure. I covered this one above, but be brave and keep your old-school landline. They are super cheap, and all your calls at home can be on the landline while your cell phone is turned off. Who knows—you may even get your teenagers to call their friends on the home phone rather than just message them! Now that would be old-school, and way cool!

SOLUTION 30

Airtube Headset. There are now more than 20,000 publications in the scientific literature that show significant biological effects from the use of cell phones.[22] As you move your cell phone away from your head, the risk of radiation exposure decreases rapidly. The farther away from your body you can keep your phone, the better. There are a few recent products that are designed to keep cell phone radiation at a minimum when you are talking on the phone or listening to music.

The normal headsets that come with our cell phones are wired and allow radiation to travel up the wire and into your head. In fact, they can even act as an antenna that attracts EMFs, which increase our radiation exposure. A revolutionary air tube technology has been developed which contains no metal wires, cables, or metal components. It basically uses an acoustic exchange principle similar to a doctor's stethoscope to eliminate wire all the way to the earpiece. The hollow, air-filled tubes prevent radiation from your phone from traveling up to your head. Dr. Joseph Mercola has patented the RF3 Aircom technology; his headset can be purchased at Mercola.com.

Put Your Phone in a Faraday Bag.
For those of you who want to be extra cautious about EMF emissions or want to go totally off the grid without hiking into the deep northern woods, I have a solution. Purchase a Faraday bag. (I like the "Mission Darkness Non-Window Faraday Bag for Phones," which is $22.99 on Amazon.) It forms a 100 percent shield from Wi-Fi, Bluetooth, cell signals, GPS, RFID, and radio signals. This is a great way to protect yourself from getting "Wi-fried," especially for kids in dorm rooms or moms with newborn babies. It can also shield keyfobs or similarly sized devices from all wireless signals.

There are screen covers on the market to block EMFs as well. I'm not recommending these covers, since the data is mixed on effectiveness and some can even cause the part of the phone that is open (so you get service) to emit more radiation trying to get a connection.

Anti–Distracted Driving Apps. As I mentioned earlier, we should expect our teen drivers to be off their phones when they are driving. If you aren't quite sure your child will heed your advice (I've been there), this is one time where you can turn their tech world on them and become a surveillance guru. Apps that prevent distracted driving will do a myriad of things, the most basic being to prohibit calls or texts while a vehicle is in motion. There are also advanced systems capable of blocking audio features and tracking your child's speed and sudden stops. This is great if you have a child who has a lead foot! Systems with the most safety features block all handheld and hands-free phone use, incoming and outgoing phone calls, texting, social media, and internet access. They can even text or email notifications to the parents about bad driving. An override for calling 911 is standard on all blocking devices, so the phone will still work in an emergency. Depending on the app, there may be a way to override the restrictions if you can verify that you are a passenger and not the driver. Many providers allow a short list—sometimes called a whitelist—of phone numbers that still can reach the driver, which is not recommended for safety, but may raise a user's comfort level.

Some phones and providers have anti–distracted driving options built in, but for other devices you may want to look into a third-party app. Life360 is one such app, and there's a good video summary on their website.[23] Besides having location-tracking services like we use, they also have a "Drive Safely" function. You get a weekly report on your teens' driving habits. You see data on unsafe phone usage such as texting, emailing, or scrolling through music. The apps report instances of rapid acceleration (gunning it after a red light), abrupt hard braking, and top speed driven on each trip. Although my kids would have revolted if I had this capability, it may work for some teens if that's all they've ever known and you make it a condition of having the cell phone and/or the family vehicle. Others that you can research to fit your budget and functionality parameters are TextArrest, Canary, CellControl, TextLimit, Live2Txt, and DriveScribe. This is a hot topic right now, so I'm sure more will be developed each month. Do your research!

SOLUTION 33

Turn on "Find My Phone" So You Can Track Your Children's Location.

This one is great for younger kids, and even some high schoolers would be okay with it—that said, I don't like the idea of spying on your kids, so please let them know you are turning on this service. Basically, you enable an option like "find my iPhone" or "find friends" to track your child's location at all times. This may be comforting to some, especially to working parents. The Life360 app also has location tracking services. What I don't like is that it requires the phone to always be on with GPS; otherwise, you can't track it. Either way, wean your children off this at an appropriate age for their privacy. You must determine at which age your child needs more independence and less monitoring, and each house is different.

Silence Is Golden. We need to closely review the daily habits and behaviors that contribute to our screen dependence. One way to lessen their hold over us is to silence our phones so they're not screaming our names all the time. "Endocrinologist Robert Lustig tells *Business Insider* that notifications from our phones are training our brains to be in a nearly constant state of stress and fear by establishing a stress-fear memory pathway. And such a state means that the prefrontal cortex, the part of our brains that normally deals with some of our highest order cognitive functioning, goes completely haywire and basically shuts down."[24]

Your best option is turn the phone off when you don't need it. Don't bring it with you every single time you leave the house. The next-best option is to keep it on airplane mode most of the time. As long as your phone is turned on, "it emits radiation intermittently, even when you're not actually making a call."[25] Airplane mode turns off your phone's connection to cellular or Wi-Fi networks and Bluetooth: no phone calls, no texting, nothing that requires an internet connection. You can, however, still use your phone as an alarm clock, calculator, or camera. Third option—make use of the disabling options on your phone by turning off all "push" notifications. How many times have we rushed to check our pinging phone only to find the notification was nothing?

Turn On Your Computer's "Night Shift." Warmly tinted screens are easier on your eyes when you use a computer at night or in in low-light conditions. Evidence is piling up that a normal screen's blue light hinders our ability to sleep well. Apple and Microsoft have tackled this issue by putting a nighttime setting into their operating system. It filters out the blue tones that trigger the nervous system to become more wakeful. The new Google release has a "wind down" color reduction mode for bedtime as well. The night shift function, once enabled, will automatically shift the hues on your display to the warmer end of the color spectrum after dark. A few Android phones have a blue light filter as well. You can also buy an app from the Google Play Store and the Chrome Web Store to add blue light filtering, but I'm not sure if they respect user privacy, so beware if you do want to download.

When enabling night shift settings, you can either put a custom setting manually—ten o'clock at night to seven o'clock in the morning—or use a sunset-to-sunrise setting, which requires your location services to be on so that your phone knows when the sun has set in your location. I try to minimize the monitoring by Apple, so I just set the time manually. You can also adjust the intensity of the "color temperature," sliding the control toward "warmer" for less blue light or "less warm" for more blue light. The setup takes just a few seconds—well worth it to save our eyes and Z's.

UNPLUG AND GET BACK TO REALITY

St. Thomas Aquinas described the classical worldview of living a life of humility as being in touch with reality. It's absolutely liberating to live a life not for your audience, or for your next post on social media, but for you. True joy and happiness come once you can truly be present in your experiences, not seeing your world through your own ego. Let's look at some ways to stay grounded.

SOLUTION 36

Shut Off the Display, Go Out and Play.
Why is it that nowadays, more often than not, when we drive by parks, the swings are sitting still? There's no chalk on the sidewalk, no kids playing London Bridge. Kids now are more apt to close their doors and open their apps then to go play hopscotch or kickball. E-sports have taken off—games that involve no physical activity, where gamers compete with thousands of fans in person and millions more online.

Katie Couric did a recent series on the National Geographic Channel called *America Inside Out.* On an episode about our brains on tech and the power of empathy, she visited Green Bank, West Virginia, a town where almost all technology is completely banned. The town houses the National Radio Astronomy Observatory, which operates the world's largest radio telescope. Radio, television, and cell phone towers are not allowed because they send out signals that interfere with the telescope. That means no cell phones, cordless phones, Bluetooth devices, microwaves, remote-control toys, or even garage-door openers. Couric noticed that the teens spend more time outside or relating to each other and to their families. And the teens she spoke to were pretty relaxed and not really stressed.[26]

When kids don't get time to just be kids and play, they miss all the wonder and beauty of the outdoor, physical world. Let's not let their fixation with screens allow them to miss all the world has to offer. Let them indulge in the real, outdoor, physical world and unplug and play on most days.

SOLUTION 37

Face Time, Not FaceTime. In the old days—as in five short years ago—when our kids had downtime, they wanted to play or get together with their friends. Now, for most kids, downtime involves some kind of a device streaming movies or playing video games, often alone.

The human brain is hardwired to need face-to-face time with actual, live people. Think of babies and how they are naturally drawn to your eyes. Staring at a screen is environmental—it is not natural. The American Academy of Pediatrics says "research has shown that it's the back and forth conversation that improves language skills—much more than passive listening or one-way interaction with a screen."[27] Child psychologist Jean Twenge stated, "Electronic communication is *not* the same as face-to-face interaction. Face-to-face equates with more happiness and less depression. The opposite is true of screen time."[28]

Kids today are spending seven to eight hours a day with screens and have very little time left to interact in person with family and friends. We need to take a break from our devices and take proactive steps to meet people in person. I'm not asking you to go back to the days of "calling on people," when a man would court a woman and come over dressed up on a Sunday afternoon to sit on the porch having tea (although, as a parent to two girls in the dating phase, that would be nice). But we need to talk to our kids, look them in the eye, ask questions, and read each other's facial cues. These are crucial skills to find and maintain deeper connections and to develop the necessary emotional intelligence to understand how your words affect people. I really do think we're at a critical stage where looking someone in the eye is a skill many kids are losing—they're too busy looking down to look up.

Let's tip the scale and make sure your children's face-to-face contact far exceeds their time on their screens. Bring back the fine art of conversation—your kids' happiness and emotional intelligence depend on it.

SOLUTION 38

Bring Back Bedtime Stories. Read out loud with your smaller kids daily, and with older kids at least a few times per week.

I love snuggling up with the kiddos and getting lost in a great story. Please keep this treasured tradition alive, or bring it back if it's not in your normal nightly routine. Do it every night as part of the Power Down Hour, and don't stop just because your child is older. In fact, if you are having trouble connecting with your teen, reading a book together at night can do wonders for gaining a common interest and topic of conversation. So much of our teens' lives is lived without us, and reading is a great way to stay connected, build memories, and have a brief reprieve from your harried days. Being read to builds listening vocabulary, which can improve your child's reading and learning abilities, which are both good predictors of success in school.

It's also important for our kids to read actual books, not just screens. Some parents link reading a printed book to screen time—one minute of screen time for every one minute reading an actual book, subject to maximum daily screen time. Reading leads to more concentration and allows our children to think deeply about different concepts. Their screens often simply present them with information or "facts." These are not the same as knowledge, wisdom, or understanding, which go beyond the factual to see relationships between things. Simply retweeting a hashtag is not learning. Eric Schmidt, CEO of Google, recently stated, "I worry about the sort of overwhelming repetition of information, especially stressful information that we're getting that we're losing the habit of reading." In another quote, Mr. Schmidt said, "I still believe that sitting down and reading a book is the best way to really learn something."[29] I love this quote from *Screens and Teens*: "I've known I needed to do less Facebook and spend more time with my face in a book."[30]

Reading is also one of the most amazing cures for our empathy crisis. When kids get lost in a book, they can really learn to identify and empathize with different characters. And let's not overlook the sensory stimulation we get with good old paper books. I love the smell of real books! There's something about turning an actual page that makes reading a real book so enjoyable. These sensory experiences are absent when you read from a screen. So, snuggle up and share a story—from a book, not a screen.

"There are many little ways to enlarge your child's world.
Love of books is the best of all."

—Jacqueline Kennedy Onassis

 **Jump Around.** I'm naming this solution "Jump Around" as a shout-out to my husband and eldest son, who both graduated from the University of Wisconsin–Madison. If you haven't been to a Badger football game, wedding, or party when this song comes on, you haven't truly experienced Wisconsin in all its revelry.

Remember when we talked about how screens mess with our kids' visual and vestibular systems? Pull our kids off their video games, and they "crash." An easy, short-term fix for this is to turn off the screen and immediately have your child do ten minutes of physical exercise. The linear acceleration will calm the entire body by resetting its vestibular system.[31] Doesn't matter what kind as long as it's linear—think jumping on a trampoline, swinging, running, or riding a bike.

We teach our kids to wake up and brush their teeth as part of their morning routine, and that quickly turns into a habit. This should be no different—wake up, brush teeth; screen time, jump around. I have given this solution to many moms who complain about the zoned-out, red-eyed, intense focus of video gaming and the subsequent crash. They have thanked me, and it really does work. And how can we complain about a little more exercise in our day?

SOLUTION 40

Preventing Text Neck. My friends joke that our kids mainly know what moms look like from the backs of our heads since we're always carpooling them around. Well, it's come full circle—we only know what our kids look like from the top of their heads since their eyes are glued to their screens. As we discussed in an earlier chapter, this constant leaning can cause significant "text neck" damage. If your child keeps their head in the looking down position too long, it can create a forward head posture that stays that way even when your child isn't on their phone. Over time, this forward posture can create a muscle imbalance from shortened flexor muscles and elongated extensor muscles, leading to some serious neck and back pain.

Here are some ideas to help you and your kids reduce the strain on your necks and spines:

- The obvious solution is prevention. Limit time on your device so you're not looking down (#LookUp).

- Keep your head and spine in neutral position with your ears directly above your shoulders.

- Use your eyes to look down at your screen instead of bending your neck. This one is an easy solution, but you have to retrain yourself. It's similar to getting used to looking down through bifocals.

- Buy a stand to position your monitor at eye level. Many are available online.

- Use an airtube headset when talking so your phone isn't nuzzled between your ear and shoulder.

- Take frequent breaks.

- Perform daily neck exercises and stretches. Some good examples are available online at sites such as spine-health.com, or you can meet with a nearby chiropractor for help. The Valeo Health and Wellness Center is a great resource—contact them for information on scapular-thoracic exercises and other stretches that both you and your children can do every day.

- Use an app that detects when your phone is being held at a bad angle for your neck. It sends you an alert to hold your phone higher.

FAMILY HOUSE CULTURE

Have you ever noticed that life is so much simpler when you know who you are? We go through life having to make so many choices all day long; the choice is a lot easier when you know what your values are; what's important to you, and where your priorities are. You don't have to constantly ask yourself "What should I do?" in each situation because you know who you are and what you stand for. That's why it's important to know what your family house culture is. Raise your kids that way, and the right decisions will be more obvious to them. Let's have a house culture for tech that's in line with our house culture for life.

Your house culture for technology is so much more than just rules. Rules may be what you put in your media plan, but house culture is who you are as a family, just like a great corporate culture defines amazing companies. The key to thriving in the midst of this complexity is simplicity. This is your house, this is what you value, this is how your family does life, this is how your family does tech—this is your family house culture. It's that simple.

SOLUTION 41

Never, Ever Sext. To many this one seems like simple common sense, but to some kids, it's really not. If it were, we wouldn't have all the sexting going on and kids committing suicide after a sex video or naked picture is passed around school. Most of us would be ashamed and mortified if we appeared in *Playboy*, and we have to be the same with pictures on our phones. You can never take back any picture you send, but it can come back to haunt you. Just think Anthony Weiner. Photos are not anonymous just because your face isn't visible—cell phones now embed GPS information in photos you take, so your location and identity can often be ascertained. Teach kids that nothing posted is ever private. Don't post or send anything you wouldn't want your parents or grandparents to see. Don't even take the pictures in the first place, as stolen phones mean stolen photos.

By the same token, respect others' privacy by not forwarding or posting a text or photo of them without their permission. If your kids do post something inappropriate, it probably means they are too immature for the responsibilities of a supercomputer with internet access. Make sure your media plan includes consequences for inappropriate use of their phone and then follow through. Sometimes as parents we have to save our kids from themselves.

SOLUTION 42

Delay Smartphone Purchase for Your Child for as Long as Possible.

This is the best advice I can give parents just starting out having children. It is so much harder to monitor their phone usage than it is to just refrain from giving them smartphones. Yes, you are having battles. Yes, they say all their friends have them. It doesn't matter. This is your house culture and your rules. Hold off as long as possible. If you don't believe me on this one, let's hear from a mom of four children who has over thirty years of parenting experience:

> *"Even the most responsible kids are tempted. Our youngest child knew all the rules—no phones after 10:00 p.m., no new apps without our pre-approval, and we will follow you on all social media accounts. We supervised our older children on the desktop computer through the launch of Facebook, so how much worse could a smartphone be? I can honestly say having to monitor her cell phone activity has been the hardest part of parenting in our thirty years. We never imagined the sheer volume of things we had to monitor because new apps are popping up every day. We had a policy of 'trust until trust is broken' in our house. But the temptation to be like everyone else online and have an internet presence was too much for our daughter to handle. We never dreamed she would get out of bed to check her snapchat at midnight. Technology itself just can't be trusted to be in our policy of 'trust.' We now shut the router off at night, keep her phone turned off and on the main floor of the house when she goes to bed, and use a monitoring app."*

I thank this mom for her time and pray this book will help her to navigate this uncharted territory of total connectivity. My best advice to new parents: it's easier to hold off than to monitor, so delay as long as possible!

If you do feel that the convenience of a quick text when they're home from school or done with baseball practice and need a ride will help you out, then in middle school get them a simple flip phone that can call and text. They don't need the internet connection and data—that is where most of the addiction and other problems come into play. I think high school is the right age for a smartphone, but I know many parents cave as early as second grade. That's not right to me, but it's your house and your rules. Just make sure you do your homework first and know the risks.

SOLUTION 43

Hide and Don't Seek—Move Addicting Apps to Desktop. This was another hack I learned from the Silicon Valley execs. Even if they work at Facebook, many of them resist the social media urge by leaving addictive sites off their cell phone, which is portable and always with them. Just put those troublesome apps on your home laptop or home desktop computer; then, when you're gone, you can't check. Another good idea: move the addictive apps to the last page of your phone app screen. It will take your brain more effort and work to find the app, which may deter you. A shocking "86 percent of Americans say they check their email and social media accounts 'constantly' and that it's really stressing them out."[32] Other smart former Silicon Valley executives are putting only vital tools they use on the home page of their cell, such as camera, maps, calendar. Leave all the mindless scrolling social media sites off the home page so you have to dig farther to find them. Some of this is trial and error, but see if this trick helps ease the dopamine urge.

SOLUTION 44

Parents Keep All Passwords. This is one of those topics that elicits conflicting opinions from parenting experts. Some think safety trumps all and having your child's password is nonnegotiable, while others think we need to teach our children to be independent and manage their own online activity. From my standpoint after twenty-nine years of active parenting, passwords and privacy go hand in hand, and it really depends on the child. I've done some things right and have learned from my mistakes, which I will impart below.

To me, a main goal of lifelong parenting is to keep the doors of communication open so our kids trust us if they ever need help. I've always had the "first call" mentality of parenting: "I want to be the first call if you're ever in trouble. If someone's driving you home and they drink, call me. If you get in a car accident, call me. If you're uncomfortable on a date, call me. If a sleepover goes sour, call me. And, no questions asked, I will help." We can't do this if our kids don't trust us and think we are spying on them all the time; then we become the enemy. They won't come to us when they're in trouble, in the real world or the virtual world. But parenting is a very complicated challenge, and you have to weigh the risks and benefits of each parenting decision to the personality and circumstance of your particular child.

Yes, we need to make sure our kids are safe, but just because you have their passwords doesn't necessarily mean your kids are safer. Most older kids know how to block texts, create new accounts, and get around the rules if they want to, which is why the main objective when we give our child a device is to educate them on how to behave online. They need to develop their own sense of responsibility over their screen activity. This takes time, and in the beginning, we will have to "shadow" them and guide them on what's appropriate and what isn't. Here are my recommendations:

Children Under Thirteen: Parents have all the passwords, review the privacy settings on all accounts, review new apps and games, and monitor who their online friends are and how they spend their time online. Very, very active parental involvement.

Children Over Thirteen: Depends on the trustworthiness of the child. Remember, privacy is a privilege, not a right.

I am using age thirteen as a general guideline. You know your child better than anyone, so it's up to you when to draw the line and lift some boundaries. Follow your intuition. I think giving a child their privacy online is a privilege for when they are trustworthy and honest. We should specifically tell our child, "I am not going to interfere with your privacy because you are doing so well managing your own space and have given me no reason not to trust you." If you have a child who meets all of her responsibilities, such as coming home before curfew, is at the place and with people she tells you she will be, upholding high standards for her digital presence, and not engaging in illegal or unsafe activities, give her some leeway. Just like you wouldn't read her diary or search through her drawers, you shouldn't need to read her emails or texts. Her actions allow you to not interfere in her personal space, and she is being rewarded for her good character and behavior.

However, all bets are off if you start to suspect inappropriate and risky behavior, violations of the law, cyberbullying, or pornography. Then, knowledge is power and you need to intervene. Your child needs to know that, if they violate your trust, things are going to change and you will be watching them more carefully. That may mean searching their room, reading their emails, seeing who they are texting, or even taking away their phone. That's the price they pay for being dishonest. It's a hard lesson, but losing someone's trust always has consequences. You need to protect your children from their own risky behavior and make sure the other children in your home are safe, without porn popping up every time they try to search for "Barbie." The message to say is, "I love you very much, but we have standards of conduct in this home that you violated, so I need to watch your activities closer now."

You have the right to do this. It's your home. You bought the cell phone and the computer. Be proud of your house culture, and uphold and protect it.

SOLUTION 45

Paper Over Pixels. Get back to the basics of using pencil and paper and handwriting notes for homework.

Since I am what you'd call the "seasoned" (a.k.a. "old") parent, oftentimes I have new moms asking me how my kids do so well academically while fitting in all the other demands of life such as church, family,

> Daniel Oppenheimer, a professor of psychology at UCLA, did a study that showed students remember far more of a lecture when they take notes by hand rather than with a laptop.

volunteering, and play. I have to say this is one of my top answers, other than reining in screen time. My kids do old-school reading and writing, from our kindergartener tracing letters and mastering penmanship and then cursive to my medical student daughter writing out flashcards to study for the MCAT. Writing increases retention. It's proven. Don't mess with it. I never knew the neurology behind this at the time, I just saw what worked. Now I know study after study reinforces this strategy.

I guess you could call this my version of rock-paper-scissors. Paper trumps pixels if you want your kids to increase their memory and recall. In the medical chapter I discussed the concept of plasticity—the human brain is malleable throughout life, particularly when we are young. The brain remembers what it rehearses. Taking the time to handwrite notes makes more brain neuron connections and pathways. The brain is just like any muscle in our body; it atrophies if we don't use it. Daniel Oppenheimer, a professor of psychology at UCLA, did a study that showed students remember far more of a lecture when they take notes by hand rather than with a laptop.[33] When people type with a laptop, they often just type word-for-word what the teacher is saying. You can't write that fast, so you have to process the information as you go, shorten it, then write it down in your own words. This initial selectivity is what leads to long-term comprehension. Other studies have shown similar findings. No wonder the secretaries who wrote in shorthand were so smart! Time to put that pencil to the paper!

SOLUTION 46

Pygmalion Effect. As we learned in the chapter on virtues, the Pygmalion Effect says that people will rise or lower to the level you treat them. We need to teach our kids we expect them to be kind and empathic, and we need to comment on it when they are. With each act and the praise that follows, they will eventually see themselves as kind people and live their lives in accordance with this belief. Many adults need this lesson as well, as illustrated in the nastiness of politics. The dialogue of our whole nation needs to be lifted. We have to just quit insulting each other and be kind.

We also need to tell our kids that we expect them to volunteer and help others. This will build their empathy and humility muscles. Our kids have so much power on their phone to pick their own games, movies, music, and social media; they need to be reminded that the world actually doesn't revolve around them. Sometimes the focus needs to be off our kids and on others. This takes effort, I get it, but guess what—the grass is always greener where you water it! Put another way, you reap what you sow. You can't plant potatoes and get tomatoes. You get my drift. We need right and moral choices to blossom to our fullest potential. Unless kids learn this, it will be virtually impossible for them to have long-term, loving relationships with their siblings, parents, future spouses, and friends. We get a real sense of meaning when we move the focus away from our own self-interest. Let your kids come up with what volunteer activities they like. Maybe it's working with youth, or the elderly, or animals. Let them pick where they have a natural interest.

Studies prove that self-control and empathy are ultimately the best predictors of happiness and success. Let's use these solutions as your blueprint to shift your kids from "all about me" to "all about us."

SOLUTION 47

Teach Digital Citizenship. "Digital citizenship" is one of those buzzwords we hear, but have no idea what it is—kind of like "the cloud." (Where is the cloud, anyway?) While this is a complex topic that will undoubtedly be discussed by academia much more in the coming years, I found a fairly simple definition: digital citizenship is "the self-monitored habits that sustain and improve the digital communities you enjoy or depend on."[34] I love that it starts with "self-monitor," as that's really the whole point of this book—to teach our kids to make their own good decisions about screen use when we're not there. And most of all, to turn the good decisions into daily healthy habits they don't have to even think about.

As parents, we are digital mentors. We need to teach our children the appropriate and responsible use of technology and online etiquette at each stage of their development. We want them to be safe on the busiest highway out there, the internet, especially when they are using screens unsupervised.

The adage "everything you need to know about life you learned in kindergarten" is a great way to explain digital citizenship rules to kids. Some rules are exactly the same, just applied to the digital world, while others are exactly the opposite. Rules that apply the same to both realms include: respect others (in person and online), use good manners, don't say rude things to people, don't bully (don't cyberbully), look both ways before crossing the street (use caution and think before you click on new links, use new websites, or agree to new terms on apps), and be a good sport if you lose a game (be a good sport if you lose at video gaming).

Then we have the rules which are opposite for real-world kindergarten and the digital world. The number one rule you learn in kindergarten is to share. That's the most important thing to *not* do in cyberspace. Don't share private information like your address, phone number, or bank information. Don't share pictures of private parts. Don't forward a picture or text someone sent you, unless you get their permission. Not everyone wants to-be on social media and you're not a reporter, so quit spreading the news. Also, don't share every little thing you're doing all day long. We don't need to see what you ate for dinner. Let's just keep more things private.

Yes, in kindergarten it was great to strive to be everyone's friend. Not so in cyberspace. Be selective with those you follow on social media. Not only does it suck hours of your time each day keeping up, but it also doesn't lead to true happiness. Real human connection and friendship should be the goal.

Last rule from kindergarten: don't tattle. In our children's digital world, yes, do tattle! Your children should tell you if a stranger wants to friend them or contact them, or if they see or hear something disturbing online. Teach your kids how to identify internet scams, spam, pornography, or predators so they can alert an adult.

Now let's put it all together with the final chapter on how to develop a family media plan and talk to your children about screen use.

Chapter VI

Family Media Plan and "The Talk"

Create a Family Media Plan. Prior to the proliferation of digital screens in our everyday life, the American Academy of Pediatrics (AAP) published recommended time limits by age for screen use. For the past seventeen years, AAP recommended zero screen time from birth to age two, largely in response to parents plopping babies in front of the most popular baby shower gift at the time, *Baby Einstein*. For older children, they recommended a two-hour daily limit for screen time. Of course, most of this was referring to television.

> All your research, guidelines, and education on kids' media use should start and end with your family in mind.

In October 2016, the AAP caught up to the digital age and updated these guidelines as follows:

> *For children younger than eighteen months, avoid use of screen media other than video-chatting. Parents of children*

eighteen to twenty-four months of age who want to introduce digital media should choose high-quality programming, and watch it with their children to help them understand what they're seeing.[1]

For children ages two to five, limit screen use to one hour per day of high-quality programs. Parents should co-view media with children to help them understand what they are seeing and apply it to the world around them.[2]

For children ages six and older, place consistent limits on the time spent using media, and the types of media, and make sure media does not take the place of adequate sleep, physical activity, and other behaviors essential to health.[3]

Designate media-free times together, such as dinner or driving, as well as media-free locations at home, such as bedrooms.[4]

Have ongoing communication about online citizenship and safety, including treating others with respect online and offline.[5]

The AAP advises pediatricians to help families identify and adopt a healthy family media plan, individualized for each child or family. The plan should identify an appropriate balance between screen time and other activities, set boundaries for accessing content, guide displays of personal information, encourage age-appropriate critical thinking and digital literacy, and support open family communication and implementation of consistent rules about media use.[6] How this guidance translates to an actual plan is left vague and wide open for anyone with children over age six. I hope to add some teeth to this recommendation and get you started on developing a plan for your family in this solutions chapter.

Notice the media plan title begins with the word "Family." To me, this name was beautifully chosen by the AAP. All your research, guidelines, and education on kids' media use should start and end with your family in mind. Guard it as your most prized possession— to me, it truly is. Nurture these relationships like you nurtured your newborn baby. Without family and faith, I don't even know who I would be.

So, before I get into any sort of recommendations, one big caveat: you know your family and your kids best. Do your homework and take these recommendations seriously, but adapt them to the family that you have created and your vision of where you want your family to go. That being said, here are my age recommendations, taking into account the newly published AAP model.

Birth to age two

No screens during this age other than video chatting (ex. Skype, FaceTime). Parents, look at them with your eyes, and do not be on your phone in front of your baby when they are awake. Have your baby on your lap, not on an app.

Most people wouldn't dare smoke and drink while pregnant; we need the same restraint when our newborns come into this world. Their brains are not ready to be exposed to the radiation or visual and audio stimulation from screens. Sometimes it's hard for parents to understand this because we don't have any problem processing screens. But our brains are long done with those critical growth stages; it's selfish to deny your baby the chances you were given.

Remember from our medical chapter, the brain doesn't come ready made when you're born. It comes with the possibility of development given the right stimulus. At this age, the greatest hope for healthy physical, intellectual, social, and emotional development is interaction with live human beings and their physical world. Babies need to look at your face and your eyes and touch their physical world around them. Read to them, have them play with boxes, bang away on pots and pans, play peek-a-boo, and touch and smell fresh-cut grass.

While the AAP says no screens prior to eighteen months, many studies point to the critical time period lasting up to thirty-six months, which is why I am extending mine further. I do like the idea of video chatting with grandparents and traveling parents, as it's brief, establishes social connections, and usually involves being face-to-face, but we don't want our babies to end up on YouTube trying to swipe at books or magazines.

Age two to five

No screens. Hold off as long as possible.

Many kids are in preschool at this age, and some nursery schools have started handing out iPads. Do your research and pick one with a no-screen policy. If you do decide to introduce screen time at this early age, follow the guidelines set by the American Academy of Pediatrics: a daily limit of one hour and only with parent coviewing. Don't make the screen your babysitter. If you watch something, it has to be together; then show them the real-world version of what they just saw on the screen. Ages two to five is the time period toddlers learn many lifelong skills, such as potty training, brushing teeth, and washing hands, and screen usage needs to have the same amount of dedication and parental involvement. That said, no screens would be ideal at this young age.

Age six to nine

No screens. Hold off as long as possible!

I still think this is too young to have a smartphone. A child's skull is still relatively thin at this point, and there are many in the medical field who recommend children should not use a cell phone or a wireless device of any type, barring an emergency.

But I do see that this is where it starts to get a little tricky, since many schools are using devices such as iPads, smart boards, and Chromebooks as part of their learning curriculum. We were fortunate to not have this issue, since our grade school didn't allow phones or tablets.

What's more confusing for parents, the AAP gives no guidelines for ages six and older other than that you should limit time and content and work with your pediatrician to develop a media plan. As you create your media plan for your family, you need to consider whether they are using screens at school. If so, it would be prudent to limit exposure at home; I would recommend no more than one hour per day for this age.

> It is much easier to keep saying no then it is to give in and have to keep tabs on the phone usage and content every day.

Age ten to fourteen

This is the age where parents are most likely to introduce educational and entertainment use for screens. Again, moderation is the key, and the majority of the solutions in this chapter should be followed to limit both duration and content. I do caution you to hold off as long as possible. It is much easier to keep saying no then it is to give in and have to keep tabs on the phone usage and content every day. Keep in mind, "No," is a complete sentence.

In addition to the brain development issues listed earlier, at this age there is heightened concern about exposure to pornography and susceptibility to mental health issues. Make sure by this age you have completed the pornography solution number 50.

Many parents cave in at this age just to stop their children from nagging them about a phone, or for the convenience of constant contact with their children. Here's an easy solution to that latter problem: just buy a simple flip phone with text and phone calls only, no data. Don't tell them it's "their" phone; instead, call it a family phone or floater, and let them be slowly introduced to the communication benefits of cell phones without the addictive audio and visual qualities of smartphones.

Age fourteen to eighteen

Think of this stage of development as akin to the baby's critical phase, since this is where kids go through major changes during puberty. Trust me, the temper tantrums and mood swings of babies and teens are very, very similar. I have included a sample Family Media Plan that consists of our fifteen-year-old son's parameters to give you an example of what a high school plan would look like. You know your child; pick the ones out of the fifty solutions that would complement your family house culture.

Designing Your Family Media Plan

Start building your family media plan as soon as possible. When your children are young, do the research, talk it over with your spouse, and come up with guidelines together. When kids are old enough, involve them to give them more ownership. They need to be part of the solution.

If you have teens who are already addicted, you need to tread lightly here; crawl, walk, and then run. Do the plan with addicted kids in stages. You can either start with the low-hanging fruit to build momentum, or pick that one habit you continually argue over and gradually scale it back. Any step you take will make a big difference in your child's health, but small, daily, gradual changes are more likely to take hold.

Here's an example: let's say your child, like many teen boys, is addicted to the game *Fortnite*. First ask him how much he thinks he plays the game per day. Then agree not to changing his time limit but to monitoring daily usage, so he actually knows how much he plays it. If you feel the time is excessive, then scale back ten minutes per day so he

> Broken rules require consequences, and repossession usually works well.

doesn't feel it that much. Keep that going; then reduce another fifteen minutes after a week or so. Repeat until it's the amount of *Fortnite* you are comfortable with.

Next, give your family media plan a catchy name, something all the kids will identify with. Let your kids name it if you'd like. Some examples that come to mind: "The Smith Family Screen Agreement," "The Smiths Tame the Screen," "The Smiths Don't Byte," or "The Smith iContract."

As I stated in the introduction to this chapter, start small and pick a few steps you want to concentrate on and build from there. For example, you decide you should limit your ten-year-old's screen time. Write "thirty minutes screen time" in your media plan, and set the timer; when it beeps, they are done. If they balk over it, they lose time the next day. Broken rules require consequences, and repossession usually works well. Maybe you mutually decide thirty is too little on the weekend and say thirty during the week, sixty on the weekend. Strike the right balance between flexible control and allowing freedom. Just make sure your guidelines are very clear, not vague warnings such as "Don't use your phone too much." Also make sure other adults in your children's lives, such as caregivers and grandparents, follow your media plan. This is especially import-ant to communicate to parents of your children's friends if they are going to another house for a play date.

As you execute the plan, remember: kids will be kids. They are going to fail. You'll probably fail too; we are all human and make mistakes. We need to just get started, be willing to fail, and then start again. If you do notice a slip-up, turn that into a teachable moment so they can learn from their mistake.

SAMPLE FAMILY MEDIA PLAN

1. Bed, Bath, and Body Ban—Your phone is not a body part, so don't treat it like it is. Put some physical space between you and your phone.

- **Bed:** No screens in your bedroom. Period. If you want to do homework on a screen, use the desktop computer in the den. If you want to stream videos, use the TV in the family room or basement. If you want to play games on your phone, do that on the main level.

- **Bath:** Never use your phone in the bathroom. This includes our bathroom at home and public restrooms. If by some chance your phone is in the bathroom and gets wet, you are responsible for 100 percent of the replacement costs for your device.

- **Body:** We don't want your phone to live in your pocket. You are allowed to take your phone to school, but we expect you to carry it primarily in your backpack, not in your pocket. When you're at home, leave it on the countertop or desk, not in your pocket.

2. Your daily screen time limit is two hours. That includes computer time for homework, streaming videos, social media, fantasy football, and video games. If you have a ton of homework on the weekend and need the computer, talk to us; we may add an extra hour for entertainment.

3. "Cinderella Rule"—Your phone has a curfew: ten o'clock on weekdays and midnight on weekends.

Your phone must be in the den plugged in at the central charging station before your curfew, and must remain untouched until morning.

4. No phone or device at mealtimes. That includes our dinner table, restaurants, coffee houses—whenever you are "breaking bread" with other people and can have social interaction. People trump pixels!

5. No phone during homework; out of sight, out of mind. You will be more efficient and remember more of your homework if it is not visible. Don't have monkey mind; do one thing at a time.

6. If you have homework where you need a device, use the desktop computer in the den or Mom's laptop at the kitchen table. Do all your computer homework first; then, at the end of the night, you can do your non-screen activities like math problems, vocabulary words, piano, reading, and showering. You need at least one hour before bed with no screens so your melatonin can be released to signal sleep time.

7. When you are on screens for an extended time period, follow the 20/20/20 rule. Every 20 minutes, look away from your screen at an object 20 feet away for 20 seconds. Also, remember to blink! You will thank us when you still have good eyesight when you're older.

8. No video games during the week. On the weekend, you can play nonviolent games approved by us, subject to your daily screen limit. This includes time played at friends' houses. We will occasionally make an exception for sleepovers if you want to watch a movie and play video games.

9. No phone before school until you are 100 percent ready to walk out the door. That means before you even touch your phone you need to brush your teeth, get dressed, eat breakfast, pack your lunch, and talk to your parents and siblings. Don't start your day with screens.

10. No sexting. Period. If you ever take, send, forward, post, or participate in any way with a picture of you or someone else's private parts, or pictures having a sexual undertone, your phone will be taken away indefinitely. Sexting is wrong, and this is a sign you are not mature enough to handle the responsibilities of a smartphone.

11. We don't want you to watch pornography. We do want you to fall in love someday with a real, live, loving human being and we don't want your brain tainted with all the fake images available online. Looking at these sites is demeaning and disrespectful to women, and we do not condone that behavior. Please do remember, though, there's nothing you can do that will make us love you any less. We may just be very disappointed in your actions and need to have more conversations about the addictive qualities of porn.

12. Do not get your news stories from Snapchat. You can take Snapchat pictures but you are not allowed to swipe to the Discover tab. If you do, Snapchat will be removed from your phone.

13. All new apps or downloads must be preapproved by us.

14. Sleep eight hours a night, and nine is even better. As listed above in the bed, bath, and body ban, no phone in your bedroom when you're sleeping.

15. We have installed the monitoring software Life 360 and Circle on your cell phone. This is not because we don't trust you—we do. It's just an easy way to make sure you stay within your two-hour daily screen limit and facilitate discussions on websites you want to stay clear of. When you reach your sixteenth birthday, your location tracking services may be turned off as long as you continue to act trustworthy.

16. You are kind and compassionate, and we pray you stay that way. Let's keep up your routine of regularly volunteering in the community at least twenty hours a semester.

17. Read for pleasure at least three times a week before bed for at least fifteen minutes. We know you love to read, so you'll crush this one!

18. When there is an easy alternative to your phone, use it. We expect you to go old-school on the following:

- Use your alarm clock to wake up in the morning

- Wear a watch instead of checking the time on your phone

- Write your schedule on the paper calendar hanging in the pantry

- Take handwritten notes at school and write notecards to study for your tests

We reserve the right to repossess your phone at any time if we suspect inappropriate behavior. This plan will be amended from time to time, especially when you get your driver's license.

SOLUTION 49

Have "The Talk" Frequently with Age-Appropriate Information. At some point, all children learn the "birds and the bees," and it's best when it comes from their parents. To accomplish this, many parents answer questions and have a dialogue throughout childhood with increasingly complex topics related to sex. For example, it may progress through the years with discussions on the right words for body parts, to the revelation that a baby grows in mommy's belly, to the fact that mommy and daddy both made you, to discussion of your body changes during puberty, to frank discussion of love, sexual intercourse, sexually transmitted diseases, birth control, rape, and abortion.

To me, tech use has to rise to that same level. We need to have frequent, short conversations with our children about healthy use of technology as age appropriate. At each developmental stage, we need to teach them information on the neuroscience and rationale behind our decisions. When they understand the "why" behind healthy screen use, they have a better chance of following healthy habits when they are adults as well. During these short discussions, families can talk over what is working, what isn't, and new apps or websites.

Agree that during their childhood, you will take the role of digital mentor as seriously as you do other important child-rearing challenges. Stay current and pay attention to what your children are doing online. For older children, it needs to be a family project and not just kids versus parents.

Here are examples of age-appropriate conversations you can have on one topic from this book, melatonin and our bodies' sleep-wake rhythm:

> When they understand the "why" behind healthy screen use, they have a better chance of following healthy habits when they are adults as well.

Under two years old

Babies shouldn't be on any screens—no conversation needed.

Ages two to five

"Good morning, sweetie. Let's talk about this new device I'm going to let you use to practice your numbers and colors. It's called an iPad. It's like Mommy's phone, but phones are just for older people. I'm going to let you use the iPad only in the morning for fifteen minutes a day, and I will be with you.

"Our bodies need good sleep in order to stay healthy. It's good to have a healthy body. When you use an iPad at night, you can't sleep well because light from the screen tells our eyes it's morning. So, let's make sure we only use the iPad when we want to be wide awake like morning."

Ages six to nine

"I want to talk to you about using your iPad for fun or homework. The sun makes us feel good and wide awake during the day. When we use screens, the light makes our bodies think it's daytime and that we should stay awake. Our bodies need good sleep in order to stay healthy, so let's only use it only before dinner time, not at night, so you can sleep well."

Ages ten to thirteen:

"I want to talk to you about doing your homework or streaming shows on the iPad or computer. Our bodies stay healthy and recover when we sleep; that's one of the best things we can do for our body. At your age, you should be sleeping nine to ten hours a night. The iPad and computer have a blue light that tells our brain it's daytime and we should wake up! It's almost like drinking coffee. So, we need you to stay off screens at night to sleep well, at least two hours before you go to bed."

High School (fourteen to eighteen)

"Now that you're in high school, we're going to give you a computer and a

161

smartphone. Before you use them, I want to talk about some basic, healthy habits for screen use. Our bodies do all their hard work to keep us healthy when we sleep. You should be getting nine hours of quality sleep a night. Cell phones and iPads emit blue light—I know it's an odd name, since it looks white. This blue light turns off the hormone melatonin, which interferes with our bodies' ability to sleep. It's like having a big mug of coffee right before bed. So you need to power down at least an hour before bed— two would be better. Try to do non-screen activities before bed, like reading, playing piano, taking a shower, and getting your things ready for school. If you do have to stay up later writing a paper or studying for a test, use these Felix Grey glasses. They can block out some of the blue light. I want you to keep this good habit up in college, so let's make sure you understand. Let's read the chapter on melatonin from this book #LookUp; then we can discuss to make sure you know why I'm asking you to do this."

You can determinate the appropriate time/age to discuss. Other big topics from this book would be dopamine and addiction, cortisol and anxiety, serotonin, multitasking, pornography, patience, and self-control.

SOLUTION 50

Pornography: Insulate, Instruct, Identify. I saved one of the most important solutions for last so it will be fresh in your mind! Hopefully, my section on poisonous pictures helped shine a light on the dark and addictive power of pornography and motivated you to take action. This is one of the screen solutions that cannot be skipped. In fact, if you have children over the age of eight, move it to the top of your list. My solution has three components:

Step one: Insulate—get those filters installed.

Get off the couch and set up the parental controls on every device you own. It doesn't matter what age your children are—even a three-year-old can click on Pokémon and be accidentally directed to a porn site. Since kids can be very sneaky, it's best to install an additional safety monitoring device to ensure no smut can get through; I listed some in solution #27. While you're at it, take Snapchat off their devices; just swipe to the Discover tab and look at a few news stories to see why. If you suspect your child is sexting, you may want to install My Mobile Watchdog, which will show every text and picture they send. Have your child's photos synced with the home computer so you can tell if they're taking nudes. Remember, we're not trying to spy—we are trying to save them from addiction and from pictures that can follow them forever.

At our home we use Disney's Circle. I love its capabilities. I can look at the app on my smartphone and see a timestamped history for each device it's connected to. Not only can I see which websites were accessed, but which had access attempted but were filtered out because of my parental controls. Curiosity is normal; if your child is trying but the filter prevented porn from getting through, it probably means you need to have another conversation at a deeper level, which leads me to step two.

Step two: Instruct.

Once you have the external filters installed on their gadgets, it's time to teach your children to develop internal filters in their own minds to protect them from the porn minefield. Lots of parents ask me how they can immunize their kids against the danger of pornography. Think of this like warning kids of any danger: "The stove is hot," "Stay away from fire," "Don't talk to strangers." We need to tell them pornography is dangerous and teach them what to do when they're exposed to it, intentionally or unintentionally.

The best resource I found on this topic appropriate for children was a book that just came out last year. It's called *Good Pictures Bad Pictures* by Kristen Jenson and Gail Poyner, and is an invaluable tool to initiate the uncomfortable discussions. What's nice about the book is you don't need to have "The Talk" before you begin the discussion on porn, so a deep knowledge of human sexuality isn't necessary. The book is recommended for children eight years and older, but many have started as early as six. Keep in mind the average age of first exposure is age eleven, and 79 percent of pictures are seen in the home, so don't wait too long.

The book teaches simple concepts about the brain and the power of addiction. The authors describe people as having two brains: our "feeling" brain, which controls our appetites or desires, and our "thinking" brain, which can put the brakes on our appetite or show us the consequences of our actions. The book rolls out a five-point "CAN DO" plan of action items for our children. Please buy it, read it together, and go back to it as your children mature and understand more. Once they are in high school, a plethora of more in-depth books and podcasts are available to further investigate the dark side of the pornography industry if you're interested. A great resource is culturereframed.org—they have a free course for parents on the sensitive topic of pornography.

For those with younger children, there is also a companion book, *Good Pictures Bad Pictures, Jr.,* for children ages three to six. Its message for the littles is along the lines of what you would teach a child about fire; stop, drop, roll, and when you accidentally stumble on bad pictures, turn, run, and tell.

Step three: Identify, name it.

Identify the name for the pictures they may be exposed to: "That's pornography!" We don't want them to say, "She's hot!" We want them to shun the naked pictures and turn away as soon as they see them.

Another good trick: if you know your child has watched pornography, have them name the porn star to take away the anonymity. Give the porn star a human face. She's not just an actress that lives in their phone. Tell them that could be their sister Emily, their cousin Lauren, their neighbor Sara. That girl has a backstory, and we need to show her compassion for the terrible circumstances that drove her to sell her naked body for money. Tell them that when they watch porn, the whole porn industry benefits and they are unwillingly promoting sex trafficking and the sex industry. Kids today have a keen awareness of social justice and inequality. Appeal to this and to the unfair treatment of these young boys and girls.

Conclusion

Those of us living today are truly witnessing history, a technological revolution no one could imagine even a short decade ago. The science fiction of yesterday is a reality, and we cannot live without our gadgets; we are getting front-row seats to experience firsthand the good, the bad, and the ugly sides of total and complete connectivity. We are beginning to see the multitude of physical and behavioral changes starting to emerge, especially in our children, and to recognize the price we are paying. If I learned one thing from doing the research for this book, it's that we can't continue at this same clip. We need to start the process of self-correction now. Too many of us have allowed our lives to

A *New York Times* article from October 2018 discussing Silicon Valley states: "A wariness that has been slowly brewing is turning into a region wide consensus: The benefits of screens as a learning tool are overblown, and the risks for addiction and stunting development seem high."

careen precariously out of balance thanks to the rectangular devices that have taken permanent residence in our pockets.

When I first threw out this book idea to some friends, I can say many looked at me like I was crazy: did I really think our kids using cell phones could be bad? I kept researching, and each study convinced me I needed to continue on my quest. A full year later, we have grassroots efforts popping up in various states to try and rein in screen time. Krista Boan is leading an Overland Park–based program called START, short for *Stand Together and Rethink Technology*.[1] For the last six months in school libraries across Kansas City, about 150 parents have been meeting to talk about how to get their children off screens.

It used to be the digital divide was about access to technology, since the rich could afford it and the poor struggled. Now that everyone does have internet access, the new digital divide is in limiting access to technology, according to Chris Anderson, the former editor of *Wired Magazine*.[2] Many of America's public schools are promoting devices with screens, while the private schools are going back to wooden toys and the luxury of human interaction. While throwback play-based preschools are trending in affluent neighborhoods, other areas are rolling out state-funded online-only preschools which already serve 10,000 children, and more coming thanks to federal funding.[3]

A *New York Times* article from October 2018 discussing Silicon Valley states: "A wariness that has been slowly brewing is turning into a region wide consensus: The benefits of screens as a learning tool are overblown, and the risks for addiction and stunting development seem high."[4] Remember what we learned earlier in this book: 90 percent of addictions have roots in the teen years. Containing screens is hard enough; with virtual reality on the horizon, no one knows how far this will go.

In the medical chapter, I talked about the similarities among screens, smokes, and slots. There's also one big difference between screens and these addictions. With the help of Alcoholics Anonymous and the twelve-step program, you can quit drinking entirely. You can quit gambling. You can quit using drugs. You can quit vaping. Maybe the overzealous use of screens more closely mimics food addiction? You can't survive without food, and it's almost impossible to get things done today without technology.

Our screens are a lot like cotton candy: they are visually appealing and taste great going down, but ultimately do not satisfy our hunger and leave us looking for something else. So what are we really looking for when we pick our phone up hundreds of times a day? Why do we incessantly keep scrolling, swiping, and posting? In my opinion, what it really comes down to is this: we are made for relationships, we want to feel connected to human beings. It doesn't matter if you're the teenager wanting to get "likes" on your post or the parent wanting to have hundreds of Facebook friends. These devices are made by people, for people, but more often than not we still feel empty because we are missing deep, meaningful, intimate human connections. That is our sweet spot of feeling truly happy and fulfilled.

My daughter was an undergraduate student at the University of Notre Dame when they had a football season made for the record books. It was 2012, and Manti Te'o, one of the country's top linebacker recruits, was in his senior year at the South Bend, Indiana university. The Fighting Irish entered the season unranked and were facing an extremely tough schedule that included USC and Michigan. Week by week, we watched in amazement as the wins started piling up. After a season of games against the backdrop of "Touchdown Jesus," Notre Dame came out ranked number one, thanks to amazing athletic talent, numerous Hail Marys, and a little bit of Irish luck. In January 2013, Our Lady's University headed to the BCS championship in Florida to face the intimidating University of Alabama. Our daughter won a coveted game ticket in the student lottery, and our family's upcoming spring break trip was moved from March to January. Little did we know we were to witness not only the biggest game in decades for Notre Dame but also one of the most surreal moments in Irish football history.

At game time, all eyes were on NFL-bound Heisman Trophy nominee Manti Te'o. The student section overlooked the player tunnel as they lined up to enter the field. Our daughter saw Manti and instantly knew something was off; his demeanor was strangely unfamiliar. After three hours of the screeching thunder of "Roll Tide," the Irish season ended with Alabama's violent overthrow of Notre Dame at 42-14. The loss proved especially humbling for Te'o, whose world was ripped apart just four days later when his secret was exposed and the rumors circulating around campus were confirmed. The sports story of the year revealed that the darling of college football had been duped by a woman he fell in love with online, who was actually a man. Lennay Kekua, the long-distance girlfriend from Stanford whom Te'o thought had recently died from leukemia, was actually an online hoax—a "catfishing" scheme. Te'o had never met his girlfriend in person; the ruse was cruelly orchestrated by a fake virtual persona on multiple social media outlets including Facebook, Twitter, and Instagram.

Why am I telling you this story? I feel sorry for Manti Te'o, who developed very real feelings for a woman he never once saw in person. I feel sorry for his parents, who were thousands of miles away in Hawaii. You, on the other hand, have your kids in your house just a few feet away, yet often are unaware of what they're doing on their devices. I know, I've been there. I gave you lots of solutions in the previous chapter, and the one overriding caveat is this: **I want you to pay attention to your kids' attention**. Remember, screen use is a business model that has one goal, and that is to capture the user's time and attention. I implore you to pay attention to what they do online; who they talk to, what video games they play, what pictures they send, how long they are on their phones. While Manti's was a fictitious internet love story, it could have been a secret pornography compulsion, video game obsession, cyberbullying, or sexting, all devastating phenomena that were virtually nonexistent prior to the smartphone. We need to play catch-up and find ways to help our children through their virtual problems as vigorously as we would if they were in person; to them, they are just as real.

I know we all have good intentions and clearly want to give this issue our attention, so why do some of us fall short? If you're like me, it's because you're too busy. Busy, busy, busy. Brené Brown writes, "We wear busyness as a badge of honor."[5] We'd be afraid of what people would say if we weren't busy.

I know as parents, it's hard to unplug when the rest of the world won't. These weapons of mass distraction are truly getting in the way of building the best families and communities we can. Remember, we're not human doings—we're human beings. We need to reclaim our lives and create space for rest. When you stop trying to be busy all the time, you liberate yourself to become something much better, to be the family you really want to be, and to have the intimate relationships we were intended for. On the seventh day, after he created Adam and Eve, God rested. We too need a rest—something we can never get when we're glued to our screens. Put them down and be present in the real world with real people in real conversations. Let's not have our kids' primary social activity be staring at an inanimate object. If they can free themselves of the hold their phones have over them, a bright future is ahead for millennials and Generation Z.

Please take this book as a call to action to challenge the status quo and rethink how your family uses their devices. Go ahead and use your phone for all the amazing things it can do—just don't let your screen time eclipse other important areas of your life. I dare you to step up and make your own parents proud by staying true to the values they taught you and passing them on to your children. I want you to teach them the art of living by showing them time-honored virtues, the skills of digital citizenship, and how to build deep and intimate relationships. You are your children's first teacher and, in the end, you are and will be their most important role model. You are also their digital mentor, a big job for those of us who are not digital natives. This is going to take effort; you cannot have a laissez-faire attitude, but I know you can do it! There's a wonderful Chinese proverb that says, "A child's life is like a piece of paper on which every passerby leaves a mark."[6] Let's make sure you—not their device—leave the biggest mark.

My goal in this book is to prove that your cell phone can be indispensable without being addictive. You can have a "Goldilocks" relationship with technology, not too much, not too little—just right. It is possible, but only with your intentional effort. This is the biggest parenting issue you will face, and you must consider the new science that is available when you determine how to parent in this digital age. You have taken the first step by building your awareness. Now, it's time we take our lives back from Silicon Valley.

We can't let our kids down. Let's all make sure they take the time to look up.

Acknowledgments

After spending a year poring through medical studies, reading books, listening to podcasts, and interviewing parents, this book came to fruition. I would like to recognize every person who helped shape this book, but if I missed someone please accept my sincere apologies. My deepest gratitude goes out to the following individuals:

To Anne Loughrey—without her, this book wouldn't exist. At a very critical time in the writing journey, she reminded me of what my career was like before I was the stay-at-home mom who cooked and drove kids around. This book percolated around in my head for six months or so, but Anne encouraged me to take the plunge and start writing. After that pivotal pep talk and some hard deadlines she set for me, I sat down and the words poured onto the paper. Thank you, Boz—there's a reason you've been my best friend for over thirty years!

To Jenny Richelsen and Tamara Sather, my dear friends who very early on brainstormed with me the idea of writing this book and helped me transfer my vision into a framework for a book. Jenny's zeal for knowledge and lifelong learning presented me with an abundance of data to use in this book since some of my best leads came from her links. Tamara's twenty plus years of experience as a teacher provided me a real-time portrayal of the inner world of high school teenagers.

To Noelle Miller, who edited my book prior to handing it off to the publisher. I applaud her tireless attention to detail, her love of the written word, her artists' soul, and her precious friendship all the times when I needed a sounding board.

To my other early readers, who combed through various chapters and provided critical and timely feedback on the manuscript: Anne Carraux, Lori Cowman, Kris Foudray, Patsy Goyette, Greer Hussey, Julie Lizak, Julie Pint, Lorraine Rau, and Jenny Richelsen.

To the many parents who shared their own personal stories and experiences with me and who wished to remain anonymous. Your firsthand testimonials of the impact screens are having on your households were enlightening. Countless insights from those conversations have left their mark on the pages of this book.

To all the moms who inspired me to write this book; your ideas, questions, prayers and support, are what kept me going. It seems like everywhere I went in the last year, moms were needing to vent about battles over their kids' phones and desperately searching for a solution. I appreciate you being vulnerable with your concerns; your candor with this issue proved invaluable. We've laughed together, cried together, and truly connected over the issues each of us face while trying to navigate this adventure called parenthood. While the subject of this book is a problem born in Silicon Valley, I firmly feel that change can be effected at the local level, and who better than moms? We can accomplish anything we put our minds to, and I have total faith you moms and dads out there can take back this control these devices have over our children.

To Professor Om Gandhi of the University of Utah for granting me permission to use his copyright-protected graphic on radiation penetration in the brain in this book.

To all those parents and professionals who cleared time on their busy schedules to read my book and write an endorsement—your kind words are humbling and much appreciated.

Special thanks to the team of young talent at Wise Ink Creative Publishing who helped produce this book: Dara Beevas, Patrick Maloney, Graham Warnken, and Roseanne Cheng. Their dedication to worthwhile causes is inspiring and gives me great faith in the next generation of leaders. This book is so much better because of the passion and skill of my editor, Patrick Maloney.

To Athena Currier, an extremely gifted illustrator and design artist. Her talents come shining through the cover design she hand-sketched, and with a quick turnaround she transferred my interior design ideas into the book you see here.

Last but not least, I am grateful to my family. I've learned so much from my children Paul, Sam, Rachel, Ellen, and Greg—being your mom and stepmom is the greatest joy and honor of my life. This amazing family of seven that we have built is my whole world. I will always be your biggest fan and I love you more than I can express on this paper.

For my husband Jim—your strong work ethic allowed me the privilege to stay home with our kids and the freedom to take on this project. You also somehow turned my pile of books, articles, and scribbles into a working bibliography—thank you! For Paul—your keen insight on the issues facing today's teens and positive feedback on my early chapters was pivotal acceptance of the need for this parenting guide. For Sam—as a teacher, you are the one most affected by this technology since you work with teens all day long. May this book be a good resource as you mentor today's youth. For Rachel—your seemingly endless knowledge of current medical information and thoughtful critique of the script resulted in some valuable changes. For Belle—my gratitude for giving us our first grandchild and embracing face-to-face time with your new baby, not screen time.

For my youngest son Greg—you deserve more thanks than I can possibly articulate. You were my guinea pig and willing "volunteer" on all the new monitoring applications I was testing. You graciously listened, learned, and put into practice most of the concepts and solutions in this book. Being a digital native, I sometimes wonder if you taught me more about technology than I taught you. You moved me from the "on the line" mentality to understanding all the bells and whistles of the apps your generation is adopting at lightning speed! God has blessed you, Greg, with so many talents, and I couldn't be prouder of the kind, respectful, and hardworking young man you are.

Most of all, I am grateful for God's love. It's by His grace I was called to name this book *#LookUp*, thanks to all the times in my life I was unsure where to turn for answers and realized I only needed to look up to Him for guidance.

Notes

Introduction

1.   Common Sense Media. "Plugged-In Parents: Attitudes, Behaviors and Role Models - Infographic." July, 2016.

Chapter I: "The Bennies"

1.   Kallas, Priit. "Top 15 Most Popular Social Networking Sites and Apps." *Dreamgrow.com.* August 2, 2018. https://www.dreamgrow.com/top-15-most-popular-social-networking-sites/

2.   Twenge, Jean. "Have Smartphones Destroyed a Generation?" *Atlantic.com.* September 2017. https://www.theatlantic.com/magazine/archive/2017/09/has-the-smartphone-destroyed-a-generation/534198/

Chapter II: The Risks: Medical Side Effects of Too Much Screen Time

1.   Koch, Kathy, PhD. *Screens and Teens: Connecting with Our Kids in a Wireless World.* Chicago, Illinois, Moody Publishers, 2015, 33.

2.   Margalit, Liraz, Ph.D. "What Screen Time Can Really Do to Kids' Brains: Too Much at the Worst Possible Age Can Have Lifetime Consequences." *PsychologyToday.com.* April 17, 2016. https://www.psychologytoday.com/us/blog/behind-online-behavior/201604/what-screen-time-can-really-do-kids-brains

3.   Bibson, Andy. "The Babies Who Suffer in Silence; How Overseas Orphanages Are Damaging Children" *The Telegraph.co.uk.* November

6, 2017. https://www.telegraph.co.uk/health-fitness/body/
babies-suffer-silence-overseas-orphanages-damaging-children/

4.   Margalit, Liraz, Ph.D. "What Screen Time Can Really Do to Kids' Brains:
Too Much at the Worst Possible Age Can Have Lifetime Consequences."
PsychologyToday.com. April 17, 2016. https://www.psychologytoday.com/us/blog/
behind-online-behavior/201604/what-screen-time-can-really-do-kids-brains

5.   Jensen, Frances, F. and Nutt, Amy Ellis. *The Teenage Brain: A Neuroscientist's Survival
Guide to Raising Adolescents and Young Adults.* New York, HarperCollins, 2015, 36.

6.   Koch, Kathy, PhD. *Screens and Teens: Connecting with Our Kids in a Wireless
World.* Chicago, Illinois, Moody Publishers, 2015, 33.

7.   Margalit, Liraz, Ph.D. "What Screen Time Can Really Do to Kids' Brains:
Too Much at the Worst Possible Age Can Have Lifetime Consequences."
PsychologyToday.com. April 17, 2016. https://www.psychologytoday.com/us/blog/
behind-online-behavior/201604/what-screen-time-can-really-do-kids-brains

8.   *Stare Into The Lights My Pretties.* Movie. Directed by Jordan Brown. Independent
Film Documentary. 2017. https://www.youtube.com/watch?v=Q5qJjNM2Kx0

9.   Yates, Eames. "Here's Why Steve Jobs Never Let His Kids Use an iPad."
BusinessInsider.com. March 4, 2017. https://www.businessinsider.com/
heres-why-steve-jobs-never-let-his-kids-use-ipad-apple-social-media-2017-3

10.   Bilton, Nick. "Steve Jobs Was a Low-Tech Parent." *NY Times.com.* September 10, 2014.
https://www.nytimes.com/2014/09/11/fashion/steve-jobs-apple-was-a-low-tech-parent.html

11.   Sulleyman, Aatif. "Bill Gates Limits His Children's Use of Technology."
Independent.co.uk. April 21, 2017. https://www.independent.co.uk/life-style/
gadgets-and-tech/news/bill-gates-children-no-mobile-phone-aged-14-microsoft-
limit-technology-use-parenting-a7694526.html

12.   Bilton, Nick. "Steve Jobs Was a Low-Tech Parent." *NY Times.com.* September 10, 2014.
https://www.nytimes.com/2014/09/11/fashion/steve-jobs-apple-was-a-low-tech-parent.html

13.   Ibid.

14.   Bilton, Nick. "Steve Jobs Was a Low-Tech Parent." *NY Times.com.* September 10, 2014.
https://www.nytimes.com/2014/09/11/fashion/steve-jobs-apple-was-a-low-tech-parent.html

15.   Ciaccia, Chris. "Former Facebook Exec Won't Let Own Kids Use Social Media,
Says It's 'Destroying How Society Works.'" *FoxNews.com.* December 12, 2017.
http://www.foxnews.com/tech/2017/12/12/former-facebook-exec-says-social-
media-is-destroying-how-society-works.html

16. Clifford, Catherine. "How Billionaire 'Shark Tank' Star Mark Cuban Regulates His Kids' Use of Technology: 'I'm Sneaky as Can Be.'" *CNBC.com*. June 18, 2017. https://www.cnbc.com/2017/06/16/how-shark-tank-star-mark-cuban-regulates-his-kids-technology.html

17. Alter, Adam. *Irresistible: The Rise of Addictive Technology and the Business of Keeping Us Hooked*. New York, Penguin Press, 2017.

18. Center for Humane Technology. Website content. *HumaneTech.com*. Accessed on November 9, 2018. http://humanetech.com/

19. Streit, Kate. "The One Toy Prince William And Kate Middleton Won't Let Their Children Play With." *KYGO.com*. August 1, 2017. https://kygo.com/the-one-toy-prince-william-and-kate-middleton-wont-let-their-children-play-with/

20. Mogg, Trevor. "Simon Cowell Says No Longer Using a Smartphone is a 'Very Strange Experience.'" *DigitalTrends.com*. June 3, 2018. https://www.digitaltrends.com/mobile/simon-cowell-life-without-smartphone/

21. Streit, Kate. "The One Toy Prince William And Kate Middleton Won't Let Their Children Play With." *KYGO.com*. August 1, 2017. https://kygo.com/the-one-toy-prince-william-and-kate-middleton-wont-let-their-children-play-with/

22. Ibid.

23. *Random House Webster's College Dictionary.* 1999 Edition. New York, NY. April 1999.

24. Russell, Kim. "Study on Effects of Cell Phones on Kids Reveals Stunning Results: Doctor Says Internet Addiction is Like Heroin." *WXYZ.com*. May 19, 2017. https://www.wxyz.com/news/national/stunning-results-after-researchers-look-at-effects-of-cell-phones-on-kids-national

25. Seger, Leigh. "iForget: A Look At Digital Dementia, Excessive Screen Time and Why Your Kids Are At Risk." Article posted on *CovenantEyes.com*. October 2, 2014. https://www.covenanteyes.com/2014/10/02/iforget-new-digital-dementia/

26. Palladino, Lucy Jo, PhD. *Parenting in the Age of Attention Snatchers: A Step-by-Step Guide to Balancing Your Child's Use of Technology*. Boston, MA, Shambhala Publications, Inc., 2015, 27.

27. Becker, Rachel. "What It Means That the Surgeon General Now Calls Vaping an 'Epidemic'." The Verge. Article dated December 18, 2018. https://www.theverge.com/2018/12/18/18147223/vaping-epidemic-surgeon-general-advisoryelectronic-cigarette-teen-health

28. Koch, Kathy, PhD. *Screens and Teens: Connecting with Our Kids in a Wireless World*. Chicago, Illinois, Moody Publishers, 2015, 49.

29. Rodgers, John M. "South Korea's Smartphone Obsession." *TheDiplomat.com*. December 23, 2017. https://thediplomat.com/2017/12/south-koreas-smartphone-obsession/

30. Birtles, Bill. "China's Government May Ban Under-18s From Playing Video Games Late at Night." *ABC.net.au* dated February 9, 2017. http://www.abc.net.au/news/2017-02-09/china-proposes-video-game-restrictions/8255420

31. Ibid.

32. Booth, Barbara. "Internet Addiction is Sweeping America, Affecting Millions." *CNBC.com*. August 29, 2017. https://www.cnbc.com/2017/08/29/us-addresses-internet-addiction-with-funded-research.html

33. Ibid.

34. 60 Minutes, Anderson Cooper correspondent. *Screen Time*. Television Show aired December 9, 2018 at 7:00 p.m. Produced by Guy Campanile and Andrew Bast, Associate Producer, Lucy Hatcher. CBS News.

35. Ibid.

36. 60 Minutes, Anderson Cooper correspondent. *Brain Hacking*. Television Show aired April 9, 2017 at 7:00 p.m. Produced by Guy Campanile. CBS News.

37. Ibid.

38. Russell, Kim. "Study on Effects of Cell Phones on Kids Reveals Stunning Results: Doctor Says Internet Addiction is Like Heroin." Article posted to *WXYZ.com*. May 19, 2017. https://www.wxyz.com/news/national/stunning-results-after-researchers-look-at-effects-of-cell-phones-on-kids-national

39. Mercola, Joseph, DO. "Google — One of the Largest Monopolies in the World." *Mercola: Take Control of Your Health*. June 16, 2018. https://articles.mercola.com/sites/articles/archive/2018/06/16/google-one-of-the-largest-monopolies.aspx

40. Parents Television Council. "Tech Safety Guide." *ParentsTV.org*. Accessed on September 25, 2018. http://w2.parentstv.org/main/Toolkit/SafetyGuide.aspx

41. Gilkerson, Luke. *Parenting the Internet Generation: A Blueprint for Teaching Digital Discernment*. Owosso, MI. Covenant Eyes, Inc. 2016.

42. Castimonia Restoration Ministry. Purity Podcast Episode 11: Pornography Addiction Help. *Castimonia.org*. August 9, 2016. https://castimonia.org/resources/castimonia-purity-podcasts/purity-podcast-episode-11-pornography-help/

43. Gilkerson, Luke. *Parenting the Internet Generation: A Blueprint for Teaching Digital Discernment*. Owosso, MI. Covenant Eyes, Inc. 2016.

44.   Parents Television Council. "Tech Safety Guide." *ParentsTV.org.* Accessed on September 25, 2018. http://w2.parentstv.org/main/Toolkit/SafetyGuide.aspx

45.   Ibid.

46.   Gilkerson, Luke. *Parenting the Internet Generation: A Blueprint for Teaching Digital Discernment.* Owosso, MI. Covenant Eyes, Inc. 2016.

47.   Jenson, Kristen A., MA and Poyner, Gail, PhD. *Good Pictures Bad Pictures: Porn-Proofing Today's Young Kids.* Richland, WA, Glen Cove Press, 2017, 28.

48.   Castimonia Restoration Ministry. Purity Podcast Episode 11: Pornography Addiction Help. *Castimonia.org.* August 9, 2016. https://castimonia.org/resources/castimonia-purity-podcasts/purity-podcast-episode-11-pornography-help/

49.   Twenge, Jean PhD. *IGen: Why Today's Super-Connected Kids Are Growing Up Less Rebellious, More Tolerant, Less Happy – and Completely Unprepared for Adulthood.* New York. Simon and Schuster, 2017, 213.

50.   Ibid.

51.   Fox News. Tucker Carlson Interview of Jean Twenge. "Have Smartphones Destroyed a Generation?" https://www.youtube.com/watch?v=DtmxKmLhY5c

52.   Mercola, Joseph, D.O. "Anxiety Takes Over Depression as No. 1 Mental Health Problem." *Mercola: Take Control of Your Health.* June 29, 2017. https://articles.mercola.com/sitcs/articles/archive/2017/06/29/anxiety-overtakes-depression.aspx

53.   Ibid.

54.   Ibid.

55.   Ibid.

56.   Twenge, Jean. "Have Smartphones Destroyed a Generation?" *Atlantic.com.* September 2017 Issue. https://www.theatlantic.com/magazine/archive/2017/09/has-the-smartphone-destroyed-a-generation/534198/

57.   Mercola, Joseph, D.O. "Is Your Cell Phone Putting You at Risk?" *Mercola: Take Control of Your Health.* July 1, 2017. https://products.mercola.com/blue-tube-headset/

58.   Wiggers, Kyle. "Experience a Lot of Phantom Vibrations? You Might Be Addicted to Your Phone." *DigitalTrends.com.* January 31, 2017. https://www.digitaltrends.com/mobile/phantom-vibration-addiction/

59.   PBS. Frontline Episode 37. *The Facebook Dilemma.* Television Show aired October 29, 2018. Produced by James Jacoby. Frontline, pbs.org. https://www.

pbs.org/wgbh/frontline/film/facebook-dilemma/

60.   Mercola, Joseph, D.O. "Loneliness More Hazardous to Your Health Than Obesity or Smoking." *Mercola: Take Control of Your Health*. August 24, 2017. https://articles.mercola.com/sites/articles/archive/2017/08/24/loneliness-hazardous-than-obesity-smoking.aspx

61.   60 Minutes, Anderson Cooper correspondent. *Screen Time*. Television Show aired December 9, 2018 at 7:00 p.m. Produced by Guy Campanile and Andrew Bast, Associate Producer, Lucy Hatcher. CBS News

62.   Warner, Claire. "7 Ways Social Media Affects Your Wellbeing, For Better And For Worse." Article posted on *Bustle.com*. May 19, 2017. https://www.bustle.com/p/7-ways-social-media-affects-your-wellbeing-for-better-for-worse-58999

63.   Ibid.

64.   Mercola, Joseph, D.O. "Loneliness More Hazardous to Your Health Than Obesity or Smoking." *Mercola: Take Control of Your Health*. August 24, 2017. https://articles.mercola.com/sites/articles/archive/2017/08/24/loneliness-hazardous-than-obesity-smoking.aspx

65.   Brown, Jessica. "Will the High Tech Cities of the Future Be Utterly Lonely." *The Week*. Article dated April 24, 2017. http://theweek.com/articles/689527/hightech-cities-future-utterly-lonely

66.   60 Minutes. Anderson Cooper correspondent. *Brain Hacking*. Television Show aired April 9, 2017 at 7:00 p.m. Produced by Guy Campanile. CBS News.

67.   Ibid.

68.   CNN, This is Life With Lisa Ling, Season 4 Episode 12. *Screen Addiction*. Television Show aired October 14, 2018 at 9 p.m. Produced by Lisa Ling and Amy Bucher. CNN.

69.   Talking Gemany, Peter Craven correspondent interview of Manfred Spitzer. *Digital Dementia*. Television Show aired December 12, 2014 and posted on DW.com. https://www.dw.com/en/talking-germany-manfred-spitzer-neuroscientist/av-17420648

70.   Ibid.

71.   Seger, Leigh. "iForget: A Look At Digital Dementia, Excessive Screen Time and Why Your Kids Are At Risk." Article posted on *CovenantEyes.com*. October 2, 2014. https://www.covenanteyes.com/2014/10/02/iforget-new-digital-dementia/

72.   Ibid.

73.   Snapchat. Story posted on Brother on 5/19/17. https://www.snapchat.com/discover/Brother/3715790678

74. Seger, Leigh. "iForget: A Look At Digital Dementia, Excessive Screen Time and Why Your Kids Are At Risk." Article posted on *CovenantEyes.com*. October 2, 2014. https://www.covenanteyes.com/2014/10/02/iforget-new-digital-dementia/

75. Talking Gemany, Peter Craven correspondent interview of Manfred Spitzer. *Digital Dementia*. Television Show aired December 12, 2014 and posted on DW.com. https://www.dw.com/en/talking-germany-manfred-spitzer-neuroscientist/av-17420648

76. Blue Zones. Transcript of Dan Buettner interview of Katie Couric: "Our Brains on Tech and the Power of Empathy in the Digital Age." Accessed on September 24, 2018. https://www.bluezones.com/2018/06/brain-on-tech-power-of-empathy/

77. Talking Gemany, Peter Craven correspondent interview of Manfred Spitzer. *Digital Dementia*. Television Show aired December 12, 2014 and posted on DW.com. https://www.dw.com/en/talking-germany-manfred-spitzer-neuroscientist/av-17420648

78. *Screenagers Movie: Growing Up in the Digital Age.* Movie. Directed by Delaney Ruston, MD. Independent Film Documentary. 2016.

79. Ibid.

80. Russell, Kim. "Study on Effects of Cell Phones on Kids Reveals Stunning Results: Doctor Says Internet Addiction is Like Heroin." Article posted to *WXYZ.com*. May 19, 2017. https://www.wxyz.com/news/national/stunning-results-after-researchers-look-at-effects-of-cell-phones-on-kids-national

81. Seger, Leigh. "iForget: A Look At Digital Dementia, Excessive Screen Time and Why Your Kids Are At Risk." Article posted on *CovenantEyes.com.* October 2, 2014. https://www.covenanteyes.com/2014/10/02/iforget-new-digital-dementia/

82. Ibid.

83. Guttmann, Amy and Evelyn. "What Screen Time and Screen Media Do To Your Child's Brain and Sensory Processing Ability." *HandsOnOTRehab.com.* March 28, 2017. https://handsonotrehab.com/screen-time-brain-sensory-processing/

84. Ibid.

85. Alter, Adam. *Irresistible: The Rise of Addictive Technology and the Business of Keeping Us Hooked.* New York, Penguin Press, 2017, 69.

86. Snapchat. Story posted on Brother on 5/19/17. https://www.snapchat.com/discover/Brother/3715790678

87. Jensen, Frances, F. and Nutt, Amy Ellis. *The Teenage Brain: A Neuroscientist's Survival Guide to Raising Adolescents and Young Adults.* New York, HarperCollins, 2015, 100.

88. Guttmann, Amy and Evelyn. "What Screen Time and Screen Media Do To Your Child's Brain and Sensory Processing Ability." *HandsOnOTRehab.com.* March 28, 2017. https://handsonotrehab.com/screen-time-brain-sensory-processing/

89. Fox News. Tucker Carlson Interview of Jean Twenge. "Have Smartphones Destroyed a Generation?" https://www.youtube.com/watch?v=DtmxKmLhY5c

90. Twenge, Jean. "Have Smartphones Destroyed a Generation?" *Atlantic.com.* September 2017 Issue. https://www.theatlantic.com/magazine/archive/2017/09/has-the-smartphone-destroyed-a-generation/534198/

91. Web content. "EMF Health Effects: Dangers of Cell Phone Radiation." *Safespace.com.* Accessed on September 15, 2018. https://www.safespaceprotection.com/emf-health-risks/emf-health-effects/

92. Mercola, Joseph, D.O. "Is Your Cell Phone Putting You at Risk?" *Mercola: Take Control of Your Health.* July 1, 2017. https://products.mercola.com/blue-tube-headset/

93. Ibid.

94. Ibid.

95. Ibid.

96. Gandhi, Om P. "How mobile phone radiation penetrates the brain." Used with permission of creator.

97. Alter, Adam. *Irresistible: The Rise of Addictive Technology and the Business of Keeping Us Hooked.* New York, Penguin Press, 2017, 69.

98. Mercola, Joseph, D.O. "Guys: Your Cellphone is Hurting Your Sperm." *Mercola: Take Control of Your Health.* June 22, 2014. https://articles.mercola.com/sites/articles/archive/2014/07/22/cell-phone-radiation-sperm-count.aspx

99. Mercola, Joseph D.O. *Fat for Fuel: A Revolutionary Diet to Combat Cancer, Boost Brain Power, and Increase Your Energy.* Carlsbad, California, Hay House, May 2017, 2.

100. Mercola, Joseph, D.O. "Is Your Cell Phone Putting You at Risk?" *Mercola: Take Control of Your Health.* July 1, 2017. https://products.mercola.com/blue-tube-headset/

101. Mercola, Joseph, D.O. "Heavy Cell Phone Use Can Quadruple Your Risk of Deadly Brain Cancer." *Mercola: Take Control of Your Health.* January 6, 2015. https://articles.mercola.com/sites/articles/archive/2015/01/06/cell-phone-use-brain-cancer-risk.aspx

102. Felix Gray website. "Computer Vision Syndrome." Accessed on September 15,

2018. https://shopfelixgray.com/computer-vision-syndrome

103.   Ibid.

104.   Rodgers, John M. "South Korea's Smartphone Obsession." *TheDiplomat.com*. December 23, 2017. https://thediplomat.com/2017/12/south-koreas-smartphone-obsession/

105.   American Physical Therapy Association. File:TEXT-NECK.jpg. *Physio-Pedia.com*. Accessed on September 24, 2018. *https://www.physio-pedia.com/Text_Neck*

106.   Shoshany, Steven. "A Modern Spine Ailment: Text Neck." *SPINE-health.com*. November 6, 2015. https://www.spine-health.com/blog/modern-spine-ailment-text-neck

Chapter III: Multitasking: It's a Myth

1.   Nielsen. "Youth Movement: Gen Z Boasts the Largest, Most Diverse Media Users Yet." Media content dated July 12, 2017. https://www.nielsen.com/us/en/insights/news/2017/youth-movement-gen-z-boasts-the-largest-most-diverse-media-users-yet.html

2.   Merriam Webster Online Dictionary. Definition of Multitasking. Accessed on September 15, 2018. https://www.merriam-webster.com/dictionary/multitasking

3.   Fryrear, Andrea. "The High Cost of Multitasking: 40% of Productivity Lost by Task Switching." Wrike.com. September 24, 2015. https://www.wrike.com/blog/high-cost-of-multitasking-for-productivity/

4.   Ibid.

5.   Ibid.

6.   Maroon, Joseph, MD and Kennedy, Carrie, MEd. *Square One*. Bridgeport, OH, Pythia Publishing, 2017, 129.

7.   Hamilton, Jon. "Think You're Multitasking? Think Again." *National Public Radio Inc*. October 2, 2008. https://www.npr.org/templates/story/story.php?storyId=95256794

8.   KARE 11Special Investigative Report. "#EyesUp" https://www.kare11.com/eyesup

9.   Fryrear, Andrea. "The High Cost of Multitasking: 40% of Productivity Lost by Task Switching." Wrike.com. September 24, 2015. https://www.wrike.com/blog/high-cost-of-multitasking-for-productivity/

10.   Talking Gemany, Peter Craven correspondent interview of Manfred Spitzer. *Digital Dementia*. Television Show aired December 12, 2014 and posted on DW.com. https://www.dw.com/en/talking-germany-manfred-spitzer-neuroscientist/av-17420648

11.   Maroon, Joseph, MD and Kennedy, Carrie, MEd. *Square One.* Bridgeport, OH, Pythia Publishing, 2017, 81.

12.   Meyer, Robinson. "Your Smartphone Reduces Your Brainpower, Even If It's Just Sitting There." *TheAtlantic.com.* August 2, 2017. https://www.theatlantic.com/technology/archive/2017/08/a-sitting-phone-gathers-brain-dross/535476/

13.   Ibid.

14.   Ibid.

15.   Ibid.

16.   Ibid.

17.   *Screenagers Movie: Growing Up in the Digital Age.* Movie. Directed by Delaney Ruston, MD. Independent Film Documentary. 2016.

18.   Bradberry, Travis. "Why Smart People Don't Multitask." *Entrepreneur.com.* February 7, 2017. https://www.entrepreneur.com/article/288829

19.   Stop the Texts. Stop the Wrecks. Website accessed on September 24, 2018. http://stoptextsstopwrecks.org/

20.   Edgar Snyder & Associates. "Texting and Driving Accident Statistics." Accessed on September 17, 2018. https://www.edgarsnyder.com/car-accident/cause-of-accident/cell-phone/cell-phone-statistics.html

21.   Ibid.

22.   Ibid.

23.   Ibid.l

24.   Ibid.

25.   Ibid.

26.   Department of Motor Vehicles. Three Types of Driving Distractions. Accessed on October 1, 2018. https://www.dmv.org/distracted-driving/three-types-of-distractions.php

27.   Edgar Snyder & Associates. "Texting and Driving Accident Statistics." Accessed on September 17, 2018. https://www.edgarsnyder.com/car-accident/cause-of-accident/cell-phone/cell-phone-statistics.html

28.   Bradberry, Travis. "Why Smart People Don't Multitask." *Entrepreneur.com.* February 7, 2017. https://www.entrepreneur.com/article/288829

29. Atchley, Paul. "You Can't Multitask, So Stop Trying." *Harvard Business Review*. December 21, 2010. https://hbr.org/2010/12/you-cant-multi-task-so-stop-tr

30. Borba, Michele, Ed.D. *Unselfie: Why Empathetic Kids Succeed in Our All-About-Me World*. New York, Simon & Schuster, 2016, 101.

31. Bradberry, Travis. "Why Smart People Don't Multitask." *Entrepreneur.com*. February 7, 2017. https://www.entrepreneur.com/article/288829

32. Jensen, Frances, F. and Nutt, Amy Ellis. *The Teenage Brain: A Neuroscientist's Survival Guide to Raising Adolescents and Young Adults*. New York, HarperCollins, 2015, 218.

33. Guttmann, Amy and Evelyn. "What Screen Time and Screen Media Do To Your Child's Brain and Sensory Processing Ability." *HandsOnOTRehab.com*. March 28, 2017. https://handsonotrehab.com/screen-time-brain-sensory-processing/

Chapter IV: Where Have All the Virtues Gone?

1. Borba, Michele, Ed.D. *Unselfie: Why Empathetic Kids Succeed in Our All-About-Me World*. New York, Simon & Schuster, 2016, xvi.

2. Alter, Adam. *Irresistible: The Rise of Addictive Technology and the Business of Keeping Us Hooked*. New York, Penguin Press, 2017, 39.

3. Borba, Michele, Ed.D. *Unselfie: Why Empathetic Kids Succeed in Our All-About-Me World*. New York, Simon & Schuster, 2016, 100.

4. *Random House Webster's College Dictionary*. 1999 Edition. New York, NY. April 1999, 1343.

5. Changing Minds.org. "The Seven Virtues." Website accessed on September 24, 2018. http://changingminds.org/explanations/values/seven_virtues.htm

6. McKay, Brett and McKay, Kate. "The Virtuous Life: Wrap Up." *A Man's Life , On Virtue*. June 1, 2008. https://www.artofmanliness.com/articles/the-virtuous-life-wrap-up/

7. Mercola, Joseph, D.O. "What Kind of Information Does Google and Facebook Have on You?" *Mercola: Take Control of Your Health*. April 18, 2018. https://articles.mercola.com/sites/articles/archive/2018/04/18/google-and-facebook.aspx

8. Schwab, Klaus. *The Fourth Industrial Revolution*. New York, Crown Publishing, Penguin Random House, 2017, 131.

9. Koch, Kathy, PhD. *Screens and Teens: Connecting with Our Kids in a Wireless World*. Chicago, Illinois, Moody Publishers, 2015, 139.

10. Google. "Google: Ad Settings." Accessed on September 17, 2018. https://

adssettings.google.com/authenticated

11.   United States Postal Service. "Informed Delivery by USPS." Accessed on September 17, 2018. https://informeddelivery.usps.com/box/pages/intro/start. action?iom=B807-82ID-USRS-PS-USP-GO-XXX-AW-XX-X-INF&utm_source=-google&utm_medium=search&utm_content=b807_82id&utm_campaign=in-formeddelivery2018&gclid=Cj0KCQjwlqLdBRCKARIsAPxTGaVm31YXHEX-z0R2hY-5mONox_Tev1mZKxeLwsO9AvcXmQgXF86PHBxoaAhcAEALw_wcB&dclid=CLDg2p-Q1d0CFYbDwAodrFEFmg

12.   Wolf, Buck. "Luke and Laura: Still The Ultimate TV Wedding." *ABC News.* November 14, 2006. https://abcnews.go.com/Entertainment/WolfFiles/story?id=236498&page=1

13.   Alter, Adam. *Irresistible: The Rise of Addictive Technology and the Business of Keeping Us Hooked.* New York, Penguin Press, 2017, 208.

14.   Ibid.

15.   Russell, Scott. "Netflix Knows Exactly How Much We All Watched This Year ... and It's a Lot." *PasteMagazine.com.* December 11, 2017. https://www.pastemaga-zine.com/articles/2017/12/netflix-2017-bingeing-statistics.html

16.   Borba, Michele, Ed.D. *Unselfie: Why Empathetic Kids Succeed in Our All-About-Me World.* New York, Simon & Schuster, 2016, xiv.

17.   FreeDictionary.com. Definition of Empathy. Accessed on November 9, 2018. https://www.thefreedictionary.com/empathy

18.   Borba, Michele, Ed.D. *Unselfie: Why Empathetic Kids Succeed in Our All-About-Me World.* New York, Simon & Schuster, 2016, 12.

19.   Ibid.

20.   Ibid.

21.   *Screenagers Movie: Growing Up in the Digital Age.* Movie. Directed by Delaney Ruston, MD. Independent Film Documentary. 2016.

22.   Borba, Michele, Ed.D. *Unselfie: Why Empathetic Kids Succeed in Our All-About-Me World.* New York, Simon & Schuster, 2016, 100.

23.   Jensen, Frances, F. and Nutt, Amy Ellis. *The Teenage Brain: A Neuroscientist's Survival Guide to Raising Adolescents and Young Adults.* New York, HarperCollins, 2015, 213.

24.   Ibid.

25.   *Screenagers Movie: Growing Up in the Digital Age.* Movie. Directed by Delaney

Ruston, MD. Independent Film Documentary. 2016.

26. Koch, Kathy, PhD. *Screens and Teens: Connecting with Our Kids in a Wireless World.* Chicago, Illinois, Moody Publishers, 2015, 36.

27. Associated Press. "'For the Bullies Involved, Please Know You Were Effective in Making Her Feel Worthless': Mother's Heartbreaking Obituary for Her Daughter, 15, Blames School Bullies for Pushing Her to Suicide." *DailyMail.com.* June 23, 2017. https://www.dailymail.co.uk/news/article-4632932/Obituary-15-year-old-killed-self-cites-school-bullies.html

28. Borba, Michele, Ed.D. *Unselfie: Why Empathetic Kids Succeed in Our All-About-Me World.* New York, Simon & Schuster, 2016.

29. Ibid.

30. Campbell, Dennis. "Netflix Show Condemned for 'Romanticising' Teenager's Suicide." *The Guardian.* April 21, 2017. https://www.theguardian.com/media/2017/apr/21/netflix-13-reasons-why-condemned-for-romanticising-suicide

31. Snopes Website. "Which Has Killed More People in 2018: School Shootings or Military Service?" *Snopes.Com.* https://www.snopes.com/fact-check/rating/mixture

32. Ahmed, Saeed and Walker, Christina. "There Has Been, on Average, 1 School Shooting Every Week This Year." *CNN.com.* May 25, 2018. https://www.cnn.com/2018/03/02/us/school-shootings-2018-list-trnd/index.html

33. Silva, Christianna. "These 8th Graders Got Bulletproof Backpack Shields as a 'Welcome to High School' Gift." *News.Vice.com.* June 5, 2018. https://news.vice.com/en_us/article/evk5zj/these-8th-graders-got-bulletproof-backpack-shields-as-a-welcome-to-high-school-gift

34. Borba, Michele, Ed.D. *Unselfie: Why Empathetic Kids Succeed in Our All-About-Me World.* New York, Simon & Schuster, 2016, 193.

35. Blue Zones. Transcript of Dan Buettner interview of Katie Couric: "Our Brains on Tech and the Power of Empathy in the Digital Age." Accessed on September 24, 2018. https://www.bluezones.com/2018/06/brain-on-tech-power-of-empathy/

36. Desantis, Rachel. "Jennifer Aniston says 'Friends' Wouldn't Be a Hit Today Because Everyone Would Just Be on Their Cellphones." *New York Daily News.* May 10, 2017. http://www.nydailynews.com/entertainment/jennifer-aniston-friends-bust-thanks-cell-phones-article-1.3153045

37. Borba, Michele, Ed.D. *Unselfie: Why Empathetic Kids Succeed in Our All-About-Me World.* New York, Simon & Schuster, 2016, 146.

38. Vocabulary.com. "Definition of Respect." Accessed on September 24, 2018.

https://www.vocabulary.com/dictionary/respect

39. Washington, George. *George Washington's Rules of Civility and Decent Behavior.* Hinesville, GA. Nova Anglia Press, 1746.

40. Ibid.

41. Snapchat. Story posted on Brother on 5/19/17. https://www.snapchat.com/discover/Brother/3715790678

42. Washington, George. *George Washington's Rules of Civility and Decent Behavior.* Hinesville, GA. Nova Anglia Press, 1746, 15.

43. Ibid.

44. Ibid.

45. Stewart, Dodai. "Dial P for Privacy: The Phone Booth is Back." *New York Times.* March 10, 2018. https://nyti.ms/2Dhi5Bf

46. Ibid.

47. O'Flaherty, William. "Humility Is Not" *EssentialCSLewis.com.* July 7, 2018. http://www.essentialcslewis.com/2015/10/03/humility-is-not/

48. YouTube. "Pride, Humility and Social Media." Bishop Barron. May 18, 2017. https://www.youtube.com/watch?v=kFszRqu1oA0

49. Borba, Michele, Ed.D. *Unselfie: Why Empathetic Kids Succeed in Our All-About-Me World.* New York, Simon & Schuster, 2016, xiv.

50. National Selfie Day. "National Selfie Day Website – Est. 2014." Accessed on September 24, 2018. www.nationalselfieday.net

51. Paiella, Gabriella. "Amazon Echo Look Is About to Make Getting Dressed Super Creepy." *Thecut.com.* April 26, 2017. https://www.thecut.com/2017/04/amazon-echo-look-takes-photos-video-while-you-get-dressed.html

52. Richardson, Clinton. *Ancient Selfies: History Revealed Through the World's First Social Media: Ancient Coins.* Atlanta, GA. Read Janus LLC. 2018.

53. Wikipedia. "I Think Therefore I Am." *Wiktionary.org.* Last edited on September 27, 2017. https://en.wiktionary.org/w/index.php?title=I_think_therefore_I_am&oldid=47582526

54. Criss, Doug and Gallagher, Delia. "Pope Francis Wants the Faithful to Lift Hearts, Not Cell Phones, During Mass." *CNN.com.* November 9, 2017. https://www.cnn.com/2017/11/09/europe/pope-cell-phones-trnd/index.html

55. Ibid.

56. Ibid.

Chapter V: The Solutions

1. Mercola, Joseph, D.O. "Is Your Cell Phone Putting You at Risk?" *Mercola: Take Control of Your Health.* July 1, 2017. https://products.mercola.com/blue-tube-headset/

2. Mercola, Joseph, D.O. "The Real Dangers of Electronic Devices and EMFs" *Mercola: Take Control of Your Health.* September 24, 2017. https://articles.mercola.com/sites/articles/archive/2017/09/24/electronic-devices-emf-dangers.aspx

3. Common Sense Media. *"How Can I Make Sure My Kid Doesn't Get Addicted to Technology?"* Accessed on October 14, 2018. https://www.commonsensemedia.org/technology-addiction/how-can-i-make-sure-my-kid-doesnt-get-addicted-to-technology

4. Alter, Adam. *Irresistible: The Rise of Addictive Technology and the Business of Keeping Us Hooked.* New York, Penguin Press, 2017, 109.

5. Ibid.

6. NewsMax Magazine. May 2018.

7. Parents' Choice: Children's Media and Toy Reviews. "The Ratings Systems." Accessed on September 24, 2018. http://www.parents-choice.org/gameratings.cfm

8. Edgar Snyder & Associates. "Texting and Driving Accident Statistics." Accessed on September 17, 2018. https://www.edgarsnyder.com/car-accident/cause-of-accident/cell-phone/cell-phone-statistics.html

9. National Safety Council. News Release. "National Safety Council Poll: 8 in 10 Drivers Mistakenly Believe Hands-Free Cell Phones Are Safer." *NSC.org.* April 1, 2014. https://www.nsc.org/Portals/0/Documents/NewsDocuments/2014-Press-Release-Archive/4-1-2014-DDAM-opinion-poll-results.pdf

10. National Safety Council, White Paper. "Understanding the Distracted Brain." *NSC.org.* April, 2012. https://www.nsc.org/Portals/0/Documents/DistractedDrivingDocuments/Cognitive-Distraction-White-Paper.pdf

11. AT&T. "Take The Pledge." *ItCanWait.com.* Accessed on September 24, 2018 https://www.itcanwait.com/?WT.srch=1&source=ECPS0000000PSM00P&wtpdsrchprg=&wtpdsrchgp=ABS_SEARCH&wtPaidSearchTerm=take%20the%20pledge%20it%20can%20wait&wtpdsrchpcmt=take%20the%20pledge%20it%20can%20wait&kid=kwd-177104108697&cid=652831120&gclid=Cj0KCQjwlqLdBRCKARIsAPxTGaWfUc-

f0rlgZyheaTye-R-uPKz5-2YFnjanisZWpQ9ZY6AIApftNyvMaAgeoEALw_wcB

12. Ibid.

13. Phillips, Catherine. "Walking and Texting: One German City Tries to Get Pedestrians to Look Up." *theglobeandmail.com*. April 29, 2016. https://www.theglobeandmail.com/technology/walking-and-texting-one-german-city-tries-to-get-pedestrians-to-lookup/article29803346/

14. Simons, John. "'I Lost It': The Boss Who Banned Phones, and What Came Next." *The Wall Street Journal*. May 16, 2018. https://www.wsj.com/articles/can-you-handle-it-bosses-ban-cellphones-from-meetings-1526470250

15. Washington, George. *George Washington's Rules of Civility and Decent Behavior*. Hinesville, GA. Nova Anglia Press, 1746.

16. *Screenagers Movie: Growing Up in the Digital Age*. Movie. Directed by Delaney Ruston, MD. Independent Film Documentary. 2016.

17. Koch, Kathy, PhD. *Screens and Teens: Connecting with Our Kids in a Wireless World*. Chicago, Illinois, Moody Publishers, 2015, 77.

18. Jabr, Ferris. "Why Your Brain Needs More Downtime." *ScientificAmerican.com*. October 15, 2013. https://www.scientificamerican.com/article/mental-downtime/

19. SWNS. "Americans Check Their Phones 80 Times a Day." *NYPost.com*. November 8, 2017. https://nypost.com/2017/11/08/americans-check-their-phones-80-times-a-day-study/

20. Brandon, John. "The Surprising Reason Millenials Check Their Phones 150 Times a Day." *INC. com*. April 17, 2017. https://www.inc.com/john-brandon/science-says-this-is-the-reason-millennials-check-their-phones-150-times-per-day.html

21. Felix Gray website. "Computer Vision Syndrome." Accessed on September 15, 2018. https://shopfelixgray.com/computer-vision-syndrome

22. Mercola, Joseph, D.O. "Is Your Cell Phone Putting You at Risk?" *Mercola: Take Control of Your Health*. July 1, 2017. https://products.mercola.com/blue-tube-headset/

23. Life360. Website content. *Life360.com*. Accessed on October 11, 2018. https://www.life360.com/

24. Brueck, Hillary. "This is What Your Smartphone is Doing to Your Brain and It Isn't Good." *BusinessInsider.com*. March 10, 2018. https://www.businessinsider.com/what-your-smartphone-is-doing-to-your-brain-and-it-isnt-good-2018-3

25. Mercola, Joseph, D.O. "Heavy Cell Phone Use Can Quadruple Your Risk of Deadly Brain Cancer." *Mercola: Take Control of Your Health.* January 6, 2015. https://articles.mercola.com/sites/articles/archive/2015/01/06/cell-phone-use-brain-cancer-risk.aspx

26. Blue Zones. Transcript of Dan Buettner interview of Katie Couric: "Our Brains on Tech and the Power of Empathy in the Digital Age." Accessed on September 24, 2018. https://www.bluezones.com/2018/06/brain-on-tech-power-of-empathy/

27. American Academy of Pediatrics. "Children and Media Tips from the American Academy of Pediatrics." May 1, 2018. https://www.aap.org/en-us/about-the-aap/aap-press-room/news-features-and-safety-tips/Pages/Children-and-Media-Tips.aspx

28. Blue Zones. Transcript of Dan Buettner interview of Katie Couric: "Our Brains on Tech and the Power of Empathy in the Digital Age." Accessed on September 24, 2018. https://www.bluezones.com/2018/06/brain-on-tech-power-of-empathy/

29. *Stare Into the Lights My Pretties.* Movie. Directed by Jordan Brown. Independent Film Documentary. 2017. https://www.youtube.com/watch?v=Q5qJjNM2Kx0

30. Koch, Kathy, PhD. *Screens and Teens: Connecting with Our Kids in a Wireless World.* Chicago, Illinois, Moody Publishers, 2015, 59.

31. Guttmann, Amy and Evelyn. "What Screen Time and Screen Media Do To Your Child's Brain and Sensory Processing Ability." *HandsOnOTRehab.com.* March 28, 2017. https://handsonotrehab.com/screen-time-brain-sensory-processing/

32. Brueck, Hillary. "This is What Your Smartphone Is Doing to Your Brain and It Isn't Good." *BusinessInsider.com.* March 10, 2018. https://www.businessinsider.com/what-your-smartphone-is-doing-to-your-brain-and-it-isnt-good-2018-3

33. Meyer, Robinson. "Your Smartphone Reduces Your Brainpower, Even If It's Just Sitting There." *TheAtlantic.com.* August 2, 2017. https://www.theatlantic.com/technology/archive/2017/08/a-sitting-phone-gathers-brain-dross/535476/

34. Helck, Terry. "The Definition of Digital Citizenship." *TeachThought.com.* Last updated August 28, 2017. https://www.teachthought.com/the-future-of-learning/the-definition-of-digital-citzenship/

Chapter VI: Family Media Plan and "The Talk"

1. American Academy of Pediatrics. "American Academy of Pediatrics Announces New Recommendations for Children's Media Use." *AAP.org.* October 21, 2016. https://www.aap.org/en-us/about-the-aap/aap-press-room/Pages/

American-Academy-of-Pediatrics-Announces-New-Recommendations-for-Childrens-Media-Use.aspx

2.   Ibid.

3.   Ibid.

4.   Ibid.

5.   Ibid.

6.   American Academy of Pediatrics News and Journals Gateway. "Media Use in School-Aged Children and Adolescents." VOLUME 138 / ISSUE 5 From the American Academy of Pediatrics Policy Statement. November 2016. http://pediatrics.aappublications.org/content/138/5/e20162592

7.   American Academy of Pediatrics. "American Academy of Pediatrics Announces New Recommendations for Children's Media Use." *AAP.org.* October 21, 2016. https://www.aap.org/en-us/about-the-aap/aap-press-room/Pages/American-Academy-of-Pediatrics-Announces-New-Recommendations-for-Childrens-Media-Use.aspx

Conclusion

1.   Bowles, Nellie. "The Digital Gap Between Rich and Poor Kids Is Not What We Expected." *NYTimes.com.* October 26, 2018. https://www.nytimes.com/2018/10/26/style/digital-divide-screens-schools.html

2.   Ibid.

3.   Ibid.

4.   Bowles, Nellie. "A Dark Consensus About Screens and Kids Begins to Emerge in Silicon Valley." *NYTimes.com.* October 26, 2018. https://www.nytimes.com/2018/10/26/style/phones-children-silicon-valley.html

5.   Cinzar, Ann. "Why I Don't Have Time For How Busy You Are." HuffingtonPost.com. June 11, 2014. https://www.huffingtonpost.com/ann-cinzar/why-i-dont-have-time-to-how-busy-you-are_b_5121636.html

6.   Borba, Michele, Ed.D. *Unselfie: Why Empathetic Kids Succeed in Our All-About-Me World.* New York, Simon & Schuster, 2016, 227.

About the Author

Judy Stoffel is a certified public accountant (CPA), business professional, author, and mother. She has a B.S. degree from Marquette University in Milwaukee, Wisconsin. Judy is a Baby Boomer with nearly thirty years of experience parenting her own Millennial and Generation Z children. She currently lives in Chanhassen, Minnesota, with her husband and her fifteen-year-old son, and cherishes time spent with her other four grown children and her grandson. She can often be found on the sidelines at her children's events, in the kitchen creating new recipes for friends and family, and volunteering in the community or at church. Learn more about Judy Stoffel at www.thelookupbook.com.

#LookUp

This book is part of the 1st print run specifically designed for the author's 2019 official book launch.